KARL FULVES

More Self-Working.
CARD TRICKS

88 Foolproof Card Miracles for the
Amateur Magician

With 94 Illustrations by
JOSEPH K. SCHMIDT

DOVER PUBLICATIONS, INC., NEW YORK

*More Self-Working Card Tricks: 88 Foolproof Card Miracles for
the Amateur Magician* is a new work, first published by Dover
Publications, Inc., in 1984.

Manufactured in the United States of America
Dover Publications, Inc., 31 East 2nd Street, Mineola,
N.Y. 11501

Library of Congress Cataloging in Publication Data

Fulves, Karl.
    More self-working card tricks.

    Summary: Presents eighty-eight tricks which can be
worked with different groupings of playing cards from the
traditional deck.
    1. Card tricks—Juvenile literature.   [1. Card tricks.
2. Magic tricks]   I. Schmidt, Joseph K., ill.   II. Title.
GV1549.F83   1983   795.4'38   83-7175
ISBN 0-486-24580-2

CONTENTS

INTRODUCTION

Card magic is the most popular area of legerdemain, accounting for at least half of the tricks published and performed by magicians. Part of the fascination card tricks hold for magicians is the fact that there are a seemingly endless number of possibilities in the ways that playing cards can be manipulated and controlled.

Card tricks are popular with laymen because laymen equate card routines with sleight-of-hand ability and gambling expertise. The tricks in this book give the impression of expert manipulation but they are self-working and can be performed by almost anyone, even the beginner.

Although this book is a sequel to *Self-Working Card Tricks* (Dover 23334-0), it is not necessary to know the material in that book to follow the routines described here. All of the tricks in the present volume are completely detailed.

The intent here is the same as in the earlier book, to present some of the best contemporary thinking on self-working card tricks while avoiding all sleights, even rudimentary moves like the Hindu Shuffle. Tricks involving complex setups or special apparatus have been avoided. The tricks here are easily learned yet they are strong enough to fool magicians as well as laymen.

The text includes chapters on some of the newest areas of card magic, Riffle-Shuffle Setups and Topological Card Tricks, as well as modern thinking on important fundamental techniques like Card Forces. The chapter on gambling contains the latest information on the Omega Bet and Face-Up Poker, two contemporary betting games.

The real enjoyment in magic comes from baffling friends with tricks. The card routines in this book were collected with this thought in mind: to provide the reader with entertaining card tricks that are easy to learn and easy to do, yet mystifying to the audience.

IMPROMPTU CARD TRICKS

The strongest magic is that which just seems to happen. If you are able to borrow a deck of cards and immediately perform strong card magic, the audience cannot but be impressed. The tricks in this chapter were chosen for two reasons. The first is that they require no preparation and can be performed impromptu under almost any circumstances. The second reason they were chosen is for novelty of effect. If the plot is novel and easy to follow, the audience will be that much more receptive.

Although the tricks are self-working, you should practice them until the working is smooth. When you feel confident that you know all the details and don't have to stop and think what comes next, you can proceed to baffle your audience.

1   GEMINI TWINS

This remarkable trick takes place with the deck in the spectator's hands from start to finish. The magician claims that he can cause the spectator to stop dealing when he hears a *mental* command.

The magician removes two cards from the deck and places them aside face up. We'll assume they are a red five and a black eight. The deck is then given to the spectator. He deals cards off the top one at a time, stops whenever he wants to, and places the red five at that point. The balance of the deck is then dropped on top of the cards on the table.

The spectator then deals cards off the top, stops when he likes, and drops the black eight at that point. He then places the balance of the deck on top of the cards on the table.

Now the spectator himself spreads the deck on the table and finds that he placed the red five directly adjacent to the other red five in the deck, and further, to prove it was no accident, that he placed the black eight directly adjacent to the other black eight in the deck. Note that the trick uses a borrowed, shuffled deck and that the spectator can stop anywhere. Note too that the magician never touches the deck.

METHOD: When the borrowed deck is handed to you, turn it face up so you alone can see the faces. Then run through the cards, saying you are going to look for two prediction cards. In fact you secretly take note of the top and bottom cards of the deck and find their mates. If, say, the top card is a red five, find the other red five and toss it out face up on the table. If the bottom card is a black eight, find the mate of this card (the other black eight) and toss it out onto the table.

Square the deck and hand it to the spectator. From this point on you never touch the deck again. Have the spectator hold the deck face down in his left hand. He is to deal cards off the top one at a time into a face-down heap. He can stop anytime he chooses, but you caution him that you will try by telepathic waves to cause him to stop at a particular card.

He deals and stops when he likes. It makes no difference how long he deals but to keep the handling simple he should stop before he has dealt no more than 17 or 18 cards. When he does stop, direct him to drop the black eight face up onto the dealt packet on the table. Then he drops the balance of the deck on top of all and squares the deck.

He picks up the deck and once again deals off the top into a face-down heap. He can stop anywhere before he comes to the face-up black eight in the deck. When he stops, have him drop the red five face up onto the top of the dealt packet on the table. Then he drops the balance of the deck on top of all.

Have him spread the deck face down from left to right. There are two face-up cards in the pack. Have him remove the face-up red five and the face-down card directly to the right of it. These two cards are placed to the left. Then he removes the face-up black eight and the card directly to the right of it. This pair is placed to the right on the table. The rest of the deck is gathered and placed aside.

The success of the trick depends on this next point. The audience does not know what to expect, so you have to prepare the way. Point to the face-up red five and say, "I chose a red five. Wouldn't it be amazing if you happened to stop at the other red five?" Now have the spectator turn over the face-down card paired with the red five. He finds that it too is a red five.

Then say, "That could have been luck. It's not likely, but it might have been luck. If it really was telepathy that caused you to stop at the red five, then it should also work for the second card you stopped at." Point to the face-up black eight and say, "Wouldn't it be truly incredible if you happened to stop at the other black eight?" The spectator turns over the face-down card paired with the black eight and finds that it is indeed the other black eight.

2 COMPUTER DATING

Computers are much in the news these days. This trick and the closing trick in this chapter use the theme of programming the cards to act like a computer. "Computer Dating" is a new effect that has not previously been published.

From a packet of two kings and two queens the spectator chooses any card and reverses it in the packet. Explaining that the cards came from a computer dating service and are programmed to produce the mate of any card, the magician drops the packet into a card case, gives the packet a shake and removes it. There is still one reversed card in the packet but it is the correct mate of the card chosen by the spectator!

METHOD: Remove the ♣K, ♣Q, ♥K and ♥Q and place them in a packet on the table. The rest of the deck is not used, so it may be placed aside. With the four cards face up explain to the spectator that the mate of the ♣K is the ♣Q and that the mate of the ♥Q is the ♥K.

Tell him to place the cards behind his back and mix them. As if to illustrate, you place the four cards behind your back. When the cards are out of sight, turn the ♥K and ♥Q face down so they are face-to-face with the ♣K and ♣Q. The setup at this point is shown in Figure 1.

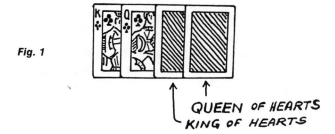

Fig. 1

↑ ↑

QUEEN OF HEARTS
KING OF HEARTS

Square up the packet and hand it to the spectator. Tell him to place it behind his back and mix the cards thoroughly. While he mixes the cards, explain that computer dating has made it possible for people to meet compatible companions through electronics. When the spectator is satisfied that the cards are well mixed, tell him to turn over the entire packet three times.

Now ask him to bring one card forward. The card may be face up or face down. If it is face up, have him note the card and turn it face down. If the card is face down, have him turn it face up and note it. After the card has been turned over, he is to replace it in the packet in the reversed condition. This is to say that once he turns the card over, he does not turn it back; it goes into the packet in a reversed condition.

With the cards still behind his back, he is to further mix them. Then hand him the card case behind his back and tell him to put the packet into the card case and close the flap.

Take the card case from him. Give it a shake as you remark that this enables the computer program to sort through the cards. Ask him to name his card. Say he names the ♣K. Remind him that the packet contains only one correct mate to his card. In this case the correct mate is the ♣Q. He now removes the packet from the card case. There is still a reversed card in the packet but now it is the mate to his chosen card.

This trick is a good example of a principle known as a self-adjusting setup. Regardless of how the spectator mixes the cards, and regardless of which card he chooses, the packet will always produce the correct mate to his chosen card.

3   THE DATING GAME

If asked to repeat "Computer Dating," you may want to switch to this effect. It is similar in terms of what the audience sees, but different in method. In this effect the spectator mixes cards face up and face down, yet at the finish only a matching king and queen are face up. All other cards are face down.

METHOD: Remove the ♣K, ♣Q, ♥K, ♥Q, ♠K, ♠Q, ♦K and ♦Q from the deck. Have the spectator shuffle these eight cards. Take back the packet. Fan it so the spectator can see the faces, and have him remove a matching king and queen. Say he chooses the ♦K and ♦Q.

Lower the fanned packet so it is face down. Insert the ♦ K so it is fifth from the top of the packet. Then insert the ♦ Q so it is seventh from the top of the packet. Square up the packet. All eight cards are face down at this point.

Explain that the spectator is to mix the cards by the following process. Openly take the top two cards and turn them over onto the packet as a unit so they are face up. (So that you do not reverse their order, take care to push them over to the right with the left thumb, take the two cards together with the right hand and turn them over onto the packet.) Then tell him to cut the packet anywhere and complete the cut. As you say this, as though demonstrating, cut the top two cards to the bottom.

Push over the next two cards with the left thumb. Take them as a unit and flip them face up onto the top of the packet. Remark that the spectator can flip the same two cards over and over. As you say this, flip the same two cards face down on top of the packet. Then add, "Of course you are to do this with the cards behind your back." As you say this, place the packet behind the back. Take the top face-down card and insert it face down between the two face-up cards on the bottom of the packet. The situation now is that the top five cards are face down, the next card is face up, the next face down, and the bottom card is face up.

The spectator takes the packet behind his back. He turns over the top two cards on top of the packet, then gives the packet a cut. He continues this process as long as he likes. When he is satisfied that the packet is well mixed, he turns it over a few more times for good measure.

Take the packet and place it behind your back. When the cards are concealed from the audience's view, quickly and silently upjog every other card. Strip out the upjogged packet, turn it over and place it on top of the remaining cards. Then bring the packet into view.

Have the spectator call out the two cards he chose. In our example he will name the ♦ K and ♦ Q. Spread the packet on the table. Two cards will face one way and six will face the other way. If the two cards are face down, flip over the packet and respread it. The spectator sees that in spite of the random mixing, only two cards are face up and they are the very cards he chose.

The basis for this trick is the Hummer-Page "Odd Color Out" described later in this book. To see why the trick works, deal a row of eight cards face down on the table. Every other card is then turned face up. Pick up two adjacent cards, one in each hand, turn them over, cross the hands and replace the two cards in the vacant spaces in the row. By crossing the hands you are exchanging the two cards.

Pick up two more adjacent cards, one in each hand, turn them over, cross the hands and replace them in the vacant spaces in the row. Repeat as often as you like. You will find that face-up and face-down cards still alternate perfectly.

If every other card were now turned over, all eight cards would face the same way. That is, all eight cards would either be face up or face down.

To see how the result of "The Dating Game" is brought about, deal out eight face-down cards. Turn up every other card. Now pick up the last two cards in the row and exchange them *without* turning them over. Say these cards are the red kings.

Now pick up two adjacent cards, turn them over, cross the hands and replace the two cards in the vacant spaces in the row. Repeat several times. Then turn over every other card. The result will be that six cards face one way and two the other. Further, the two cards will be the red kings.

4   PENNY PLAIN

This is a card revelation done under seemingly impossible conditions. It is the author's handling of a principle first published by Alex Elmsley.

Have a spectator take his own deck and deal two heaps containing the same number of cards. He shuffles one heap, notes the top card and places the heap on the table. Then he shuffles the other heap and places that on top of the first heap, thus burying the chosen card somewhere in the packet.

Another spectator is asked to guess where he thinks the chosen card will end up. If he thinks the card will end up twelfth from the top, he deals 12 cards off the deck onto the tabled packet. He does this while you turn your back. You have no idea of how many cards he dealt.

Now you take the packet, grasping it from above in the right hand. The left thumb draws the top card off while the fingers of the left hand simultaneously draw the bottom card off as shown in Figure 2. This pair of cards is placed on the table.

Fig. 2

Draw off another pair of cards in the same way and place them onto the tabled cards. Continue drawing off pairs of cards until all of the cards have been drawn off and placed onto the tabled cards. Then place the top card at the bottom of the packet. This transfer of a card from top to bottom is done openly.

Ask the spectator for his number. In our example he would say 12. Deal 12 cards off the top of the packet. Turn over the next card and it will be the chosen card.

5 MIRASKIL

The invention of Stewart James, Miraskil is a classic of modern card magic. The following version was devised by Joseph K. Schmidt and the author. The only requirements are a deck of 52 cards and a slip of paper.

On the paper write, "You will end up with four more face-down cards than face-up cards." Fold the paper and drop it into a drinking glass so it is in plain view.

Remove the deck from its case and silently deal 28 cards off the top. Turn the balance of the deck face up and shuffle face-up cards into face-down cards. Square up the deck and place it before a spectator.

Invite him to shuffle the deck until he is satisfied it is completely mixed. When he has done this, pretend to study the deck. Then pretend to make a mental calculation. Nod as if satisfied, then say, "Give the deck one more shuffle and it should work."

He is now to deal the cards two at a time off the top. If the dealt pair contains two face-down cards, he places them in a heap to the left. If both cards are face up he deals them into a separate heap to the right. If he deals a pair which contain one face-up card and one face-down card, he deals them into a pile in the center.

The spectator deals pairs of cards until he has gone through the entire deck. He will have three heaps of cards on the table: one consisting of face-down cards, one of face-up cards, and one a mixture of face-up and face-down cards. Have him count aloud the number of cards in the face-down heap. Then have him count aloud the number of cards in the face-up heap. When he reads the prediction he will find that it is correct. There are four more face-down cards than face-up.

There is a simple way to repeat the trick so that the outcome is different. When the spectator counts the cards in the face-up heap and the face-down heap, pick up the heap containing the mixture of face-up and face-down cards. Cut it and complete the cut so there is a face-up card on top of this heap. The right hand takes this card, places it under the heap, and uses it to scoop up the heap and flip it over into the waiting left hand, as in Figure 3.

Fig. 3

Then place the face-up card on top of the heap and immediately give this heap a riffle shuffle. The handling allowed you to turn over the heap but not the card used as a scoop.

To repeat the trick, shuffle the face-down heap into this heap, then shuffle the face-up heap into this heap. Hand the deck to the spectator for further shuffling. On a separate slip of paper write, "You will end up with two more face-down cards than face-up cards."

Have the spectator shuffle the deck and deal the cards into three heaps as described above. Then have him open the prediction slip. Once again the prediction is correct.

6 THE SEVEN-UP MYSTERY

Impromptu mental effects are invaluable on those occasions when you are handed a deck of cards and want to impress people with your mind-reading abilities. This routine smacks of mentalism but in fact it's based on a simple premise.

The trick is introduced as the Seven-Up Trick. Before anything else is done you explain that the trick gets its name from the fact that you will later spell "Seven Up" to arrive at the chosen card.

Note that at the very beginning of the routine you've told the audience what you intend to do. This would seem to eliminate the possibility of cheating later on but there are ways and ways of spelling "Seven Up."

The spectator is given a packet of 13 cards. While you turn your back the spectator shuffles the packet and notes the face (or bottom) card. Whatever that card is, he mentally spells the suit, transferring a card for each letter from top to bottom. If for example the card was the ♣7, he would spell C-L-U-B-S, and silently transfer a card for each letter from top to bottom.

Take the packet and state that you will try to find his card. Place the packet below the level of the tabletop or behind your back. With the cards out of sight, count down to the fifth card, turn it face up and exchange it for the bottom card of the packet. Bring the packet into view. Ask for the name of the chosen card. Depending on the suit, proceed as follows:

If the spectator's card was a club, spell "Seven Up," dealing a card for each letter from top to bottom. When you've completed the deal, turn over the next card and it will be the selected card.

If the spectator names hearts or spades, spell "Seven Up," dealing a card for each letter from top to bottom. Turn up the last card dealt and show it to be the chosen card.

If the spectator names diamonds, spell "Seven," transferring a card for each letter. Then pause and say, "We spell *seven* and your card turns *up*." Spread the cards to show the chosen card face up in the center of the spread.

It is true that there will be a face-up card in the packet if the spectator's card is anything other than a diamond, but this should give you no trouble. At the conclusion of the trick simply place the packet on top of the deck, cut the deck and complete the cut. If a face-up card is later spotted in the deck it will never be connected with the Seven-Up Trick.

7 THE OPEN PREDICTION

A card problem suggested by Paul Curry has become a classic in contemporary card magic. The effect appears to be impossible. As seen by the audience, the magician writes a prediction on a slip of paper and places the paper in full view. The prediction, which can be seen by all present, reads: "You will choose the ace of spades," for example. Note that the prediction is known at the start, making it impossible for the magician to change his mind or switch predictions.

The spectator is given a deck of cards. He deals cards off the top one at a time into a face-up heap on the table. At some point he deals one card face down. Then he deals the rest of the deck face up. As he deals he is asked to look for the ♠A among the face-up cards. The ♠A never shows up. There is one face-down card on the table. It is the only card the spectator did not turn face up. When the spectator turns this card over, he sees that it is the ♠A, the very card predicted by the magician.

Many solutions to this card problem have been proposed. The following, based on ideas of Lin Searles and Ed Balducci, is one of the simplest. The magician never touches the deck once the prediction is written.

METHOD: Take any well-shuffled deck and look through it as if to study the cards. Say you are going to try to guess where the spectator is going to stop. All you really do is note the top card of the deck. We will assume it is the ♠A. Square up the deck, place it face down on the table and write the prediction mentioned above. Make sure the spectators see exactly what you write.

Hand the deck to the spectator. Tell him to cut off about a third of the deck, turn it face up and place it on top of the rest of the pack. When he has done this, instruct him to cut off about two-thirds of the deck, turn this portion over and place it on top of the balance of the deck. If correctly done, there will now be a face-up portion on top followed by a face-down portion.

Tell the spectator to deal the face-up cards off the deck into a face-up heap, dealing one card at a time. Instruct him to deal the first face-down card off the deck so it is kept face down and no one sees its face. Then have him turn over each of the other face-down cards in the deck. At the finish there will be one face-down card. The rest of the deck is face-up.

It appears as if the face-down card was selected by a completely random process, but it will be the ♠A. Have the spectator turn this card over to show it matches your prediction.

8 FLIP TOP

In this classic effect the deck is tossed face down onto the table, whereupon an ace turns face up on top of the deck. Although the effect is well known among magicians, the correct technique is not.

We will cover the technique first and then extend the principle to a number of previously unpublished applications.

Begin with any ace on top of the deck. The card can be any card but aces are more dramatic. Hold the deck face down in the left-hand dealing position. As the right hand picks up the deck from above, the left thumb pushes the top card to the right about an inch as shown in Figure 4. This is done as the hands are raised above eye level. The action is covered by the right hand, which is above the deck at this point as shown in Figure 5. The right hand then holds the deck about 18 inches above the tabletop. The deck is parallel to the table. It is best when learning the technique to have a tablecloth covering the table because the soft surface will absorb the impact and the cards won't scatter.

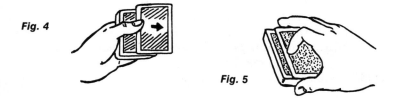

Fig. 4

Fig. 5

If you drop the deck, the ace will turn over because it is offset over the side of the deck and air pressure will cause it to flip face up. But if you just drop the deck, the ace will turn over at the last instant, making it obvious to the audience what happened. Instead of dropping the deck, toss it gently. The ace will flip over faster and the effect will appear magical.

After you try the effect a few times, you may want to consider a variation. The left thumb does not push the top card over to the right as in Figure 4. Instead, the fingers of the left hand slide under the deck and push the bottom card to the right, as in Figure 6. As before, the right hand is above the deck and covers the action.

Fig. 6

You will have to push the bottom card over about 1½ inches. Otherwise the technique is the same. Work on a soft surface (either a tablecloth or a rug) until you get the knack. A simple application is to have an ace on top and bottom of the deck. Perform the first technique to cause the topmost ace to turn face up as you toss the deck onto the table. Leave that ace squared and still face up on top of the deck as you pick up the deck and replace it in the left hand. Then use the second technique to cause the bottom card of the deck to turn face up. This will puzzle those who know or suspect the first method.

A subtle application is the following. Secretly reverse the bottom card of the deck. Have the spectator choose a card. Then tell him to place it on top of the pack. Use the technique of Figure 6 to get the deck ready to flip over the bottom card. Toss the deck onto the table. A card will fly off the deck face down.

Say, "Your card was supposed to turn over. Let me try that again." Place the face-down card in the center of the deck, acting as if *this* card is his card. Then perform the technique of Figure 4 to get the deck ready to flip over the top card. Toss the deck onto the table. It will appear as if his card slid out of the center of the deck, turned face up and landed on top.

9   TELEVISION DICE

It is well known that the picture you see on a television screen is really a series of images. If the set is turned off, an image will remain on the screen for a fraction of a second and then dissolve. Images can be captured in a variety of ways, some of them most mysterious.

The magician drops two dice onto the table. While he turns his back he asks the spectator to roll the dice several times to verify they are not loaded. Then the spectator rolls the dice one final time.

He notes the topmost number on one die. Say it is four. He picks up any shuffled deck of cards and notes the card fourth from the top. The deck is given to the magician behind his back. The chosen die is hidden under a cup.

The magician turns around and faces the spectator. "There is one die on the table," he says. "Obviously it can't give me any information because you chose a card by means of the die hidden under the cup. Still, the die on the table contains a mental image of what number showed on the other die. Sometimes one can pick up impressions."

With the deck behind his back the magician studies the visible die, then makes an adjustment to the cards. Then he places the deck on the table. "Without looking at the deck I was able to find your card and place it in a new location," he says. "For the first time, uncover the die you used."

The cup is lifted. The number on top of the die is four. "You threw a four on this die and a six on this die," the magician says. "The total is ten, right?"

The spectator agrees. "Count down to the tenth card," the magician says. The spectator counts ten cards, turns up the next card and discovers that it is his previously chosen card.

METHOD: The trick is a swindle. The visible die on the table does indeed tell the magician all he needs to know, but in an offbeat way. When the magician gets the deck behind his back he turns and faces the spectator. Whatever number shows on the visible die, he transfers that many cards from the bottom to the top of the deck. Then he transfers one more card. In our example a six would show on the visible die. The magician transfers six cards from bottom to top, then one more card. The deck is then handed to the spectator.

He uncovers the chosen die. The uppermost numbers on the two dice are added together. The spectator counts down that many cards, turns up the next card and discovers it is his chosen card.

10 DECKSPERT

If asked to repeat the above trick on another occasion, and four dice are available, you can perform an even stronger version of "Television Dice." The presentation angle was taken from a routine of Stewart James.

If possible use dice of two different colors, say two red and two green. This is not strictly necessary to the working but it adds to the mystery. While your back is turned a spectator rolls all four dice. He chooses one color. We'll assume he picks red. Mentally he adds together the top numbers on the two red dice. Then he notes a card at the corresponding position from the top of his deck of cards. If he rolled three on one die and six on the other, he would add these numbers together, getting nine, and note the card that is ninth from the top of the deck. Once he has done this he covers the two red dice.

The deck is handed to you behind your back. Turn and face the spectator. Glance at the white dice and note the topmost numbers. Say these numbers are a three and a two. Mentally add them together, getting five. Subtract five from 28 (the sum is always subtracted from 28). Whatever number you get, deal that many cards off the top of the deck. Deal one card at a time and deal each card onto the last, thus reversing the order. The cards are dealt from the left hand into the right hand. When you finish the deal, place the dealt cards back onto the top of the deck.

The intriguing part of the routine comes in at this point. Place the deck on the table in full view. Then have the spectator uncover the two red dice. Tell him to turn all four dice over to bring new numbers uppermost. Then have him point to one of the dice. Say he points to a die with the number four uppermost. Deal four cards off the top into a heap on the table. Then the spectator points to another die. Say it shows a one uppermost. Deal one card onto the tabled heap. Continue in this way with the other two dice. The spectator can point to the dice in any order. When you have dealt cards corresponding to the top number on each of the four dice, turn over the top card and it will be the chosen card.

If dice are not available there is an impromptu substitute. Using a paper clip, attach a three back-to-back with a four. Then attach a one (ace) back-to-back with a six. Then attach a two back-to-back with a five. Repeat this same procedure with the remaining aces through sixes. The result will be that you have 12 pairs of cards. The spectator may mix the pairs and choose any four pairs. Proceed from here with the trick exactly as written.

11   CRAZY CLOCKS

Novel effects are always remembered by the audience. Fred Taylor here describes an offbeat trick that originally appeared in a European magazine. The magician writes a prediction, folds it and places it under the spectator's watchband for safekeeping. The spectator is asked to think of any full hour from one to 12. When he has an hour in mind, 12 cards are dealt off the pack face up and arranged in the form of a clock dial as shown in Figure 7.

The spectator is asked to remember the card that appears at the position of his thought-of hour. The performer correctly reveals the hour. Then the prediction is removed from under the spectator's

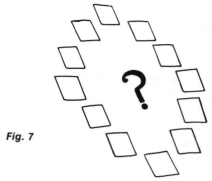

Fig. 7

watchband, opened and read aloud. The performer has correctly predicted the card chosen by the spectator.

The trick may be immediately repeated without the performer going near the deck.

METHOD: Go through the deck and remark that you want to discard any jokers that might be in the pack. As you look through the cards note and remember the thirteenth and twenty-fifth cards from the top of the pack. Say the thirteenth card is the ♣4 and the twenty-fifth card the ♦8. The ♣4 will be the first card you predict.

Place the deck face down on the table. On a slip of paper write, "You will choose the ♣4." Fold the slip and have the spectator place it under his watchband for the time being. Now have the spectator mentally decide on any hour between one and 12. Have him look at his watch when he does this, and say that the slip of paper might influence his choice by telepathic suggestion.

Turn your back. The spectator is to deal off the top of the deck a number of cards corresponding to his thought-of number. If, say, he thought of five o'clock, he would deal five cards off the top of the deck. He places these five cards in his pocket so the magician has no clue as to the number dealt.

The magician then takes the deck and deals 12 cards to represent a clock face. The cards are first dealt singly into a heap on the table. Then they are placed around an imaginary clock face, beginning at the one o'clock position, the cards being arranged face up. Mentally note the position of the previously noted thirteenth card, the ♣4 in our example, and you know the selected hour. Jot this on a second slip of paper.

Have the spectator announce the chosen hour. He then notes the card at that hour on the clock face. In our example he would note the card at the five o'clock position. This card will be the ♣4. Have him open the second slip, which correctly indicates the hour he thought of. Then have him open the slip under his watchband. He will discover that you correctly predicted which card he would choose.

The cards representing the clock face are placed aside. The cards in the spectator's pocket are added to the top of the deck. You are now ready for an immediate repeat without going near the deck. On a sheet of paper write, "You will take the ♦8." Fold the slip, place it under the spectator's watchband, and proceed with the trick exactly as you did the first time.

12 TO LIE OR TELL THE TRUTH

Jack Avis devised an excellent trick which will quickly establish your reputation as a card expert. The plot, originally suggested by Martin Gardner, is one where the spectator is asked a series of questions about a chosen card and is encouraged to lie or tell the truth in answer to the questions. The deck has been programmed like a lie detector. It provides the correct answers to his questions, and then it goes on to produce the chosen card!

It is only necessary that you secretly note the bottom card of the deck before the trick begins. This can be done under cover of the excuse that you want to check that the deck contains 52 cards. Simply glimpse the bottom card while you count the cards. The glimpsed card becomes your key card.

Spread the deck face down and have the spectator remove any card. He notes the card, puts the card on top of the deck, then cuts the deck and completes the cut. Take back the deck. Turn it face up, spread it from left to right, find your key card, and note the card just to the right of it. This will be the spectator's chosen card. Cut the deck between the key card and the chosen card. Complete the cut. His card will now be on top.

You're now going to make a series of setting-up moves. While doing this, tell the spectator you are programming the deck to act like a lie detector, and that once programmed it is infallible and will produce the right answer no matter how he tries to trick it with false answers. Once the deck has been programmed you will invite the spectator to assist, and he is to try to beat the lie detector by giving it incorrect information. In other words, he may lie or tell the truth in answer to your questions.

The setting-up process is given here. It will take a bit of practice to get it to the point where it can be done smoothly and quickly. The deck is face up and you have cut the chosen card to the top of the deck. From the *face* of the deck and working to the *left,* upjog cards as follows:

> One card of the same *value* as the selected card.
> Three indifferent cards.
> Two cards of the same *suit* as the selected card.
> Three indifferent cards.
> One card of the same *color* as the selected card.
> One indifferent card.
> One card of the same *color* as the selected card.
> Two indifferent cards.

As an example, assume the spectator chose the ♣K. Beginning at the face of the deck and working to the left, upjog a king, then three indifferent cards, then two clubs, then three more indifferent cards, then a black card, then an indifferent card, then two black cards, and finally two indifferent cards.

Retain the deck in the right hand. With the left hand strip out the jogged cards as a unit, and allow them to drop into the left palm. Drop the deck on top of the cards in the left hand, square up the pack and turn it face down.

Ask the spectator if his card was red or black. Remind him that he can lie in answer to this and every other question. The idea is to trick the lie detector. Whatever his answer, spell it out a card at a time, forming a small packet. If for example he answers red, spell "R-E-D," dealing a card for each letter, forming a three-card packet.

The second question has to do with suit. If he said his card was red, now ask if it was hearts or a diamond. If in answer to the first question he said his card was black, now ask if it was clubs or a spade. Spell out his answer, forming a second packet to the right of the first packet.

The third and final question has to do with the value of the chosen card. Ask, "Was the card a court card or did it have spots?" As with each of the other two questions, the spectator may lie or tell the truth when answering. Spell C-O-U-R-T or S-P-O-T-S, whichever he chooses, in answer to the third question, dealing these cards into a third packet to the right of the other two.

Now say, "You've done your best to fool the lie detector. Let's see what the real truth is." Working from left to right, turn up the top card of each packet. Your patter might run like this: "The computerized lie detector indicates that you chose a red card. It was a diamond. It was a court card. In fact this is your chosen card."

If the spectator chose hearts, the selected card will be on top of the deck at the finish. When you get to the line, "In fact this is your chosen card," turn up the top card of the pack. In all other cases the chosen card will be the top card of the third packet.

The spelling must be done exactly as described above. Master the details of this fine routine and you will have in your possession a truly baffling card trick.

RED-BLACK MYSTERIES

John N. Hilliard once observed, "The great majority of card tricks begin with a spectator choosing a card which he notes and then replaces in the deck. That card is then discovered and revealed by the magician in various ways."

It is wise to have on hand tricks which depend on a different plot idea. In this way the audience can be entertained with a wide variety of different card effects. Tricks involving reds and blacks are ideal because the effects are novel and quite different from card locations. This chapter describes some of the best contemporary mysteries with reds and blacks.

13 CHROMATIC CAPER

The only requirements for this unusual trick are a deck of cards and two slips of paper. Have the spectator shuffle the deck and deal it into two heaps of 26 cards each. Then tell him to turn either half of the deck face up and shuffle it into the face-down half of the pack. Let him give the deck two or three shuffles.

Ask him to name two of the suits. Point out that there are 12 answers he can give (clubs-hearts, spades-hearts, clubs-diamonds, etc.) and that you could have no way of guessing ahead of time which two suits he will choose. He might choose clubs and hearts. Jot these down on a slip of paper and place it before the spectator. Jot down the remaining two suits (spades and diamonds in our example) on the remaining slip and place this slip near you. The only reason for the slips is to remind the spectator of the two suits he freely chose for himself.

While you fill out the slips, have the spectator deal the deck into two heaps of 26 cards each. When he has done this, have him pick up one heap, go through it and remove the face-up cards of the suits he has chosen—clubs and hearts is our example. After these cards have been removed, take the remainder of the heap from him, turn it over and place it on the table.

Then have the spectator go through the other heap and similarly remove all the face-up clubs and hearts. He adds these to the clubs and hearts removed from the other half of the deck. When he has done this, take the remainder of the heap from him, turn it over and place it near the first heap. The situation is now as in Figure 8. There is a packet containing face-up clubs and hearts. Below it are two heaps containing a mixture of face-up and face-down cards.

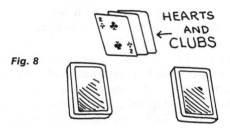

HEARTS
AND
CLUBS

Fig. 8

Remind the spectator that he chose any two suits for himself and left the other two suits for you. Go through each of the heaps, remove all the face-up spades and diamonds, and place them in front of you. The situation now looks like Figure 9.

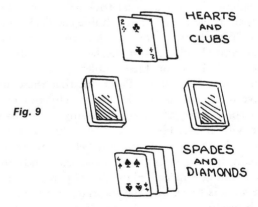

HEARTS
AND
CLUBS

Fig. 9

SPADES
AND
DIAMONDS

Have the spectator count the clubs and hearts in his packet. Then have him count the spades and diamonds in your packet. He will be surprised to discover that you have exactly as many cards in your packet as he has in his.

For the final surprise gather the balance of the two remaining heaps and spread them on the table to reveal that the *only* face-up cards in them are clubs and hearts, the two suits freely chosen by the spectator!

14 FLYING COLORS

The spectator gives an ordinary deck of cards a riffle shuffle. He then divides the deck into two heaps and gives the deck another shuffle. The magician removes a red card and a black card from the middle of the deck. Passing these cards over the deck, he causes all the reds to separate from all the blacks. The colors separate instantly, a startling trick in view of the fact that the deck was given repeated shuffles by the spectator.

METHOD: This routine is based on an idea of George Pierce and Charles Jordan. Beforehand place 13 red cards face down on the table. Place 13 blacks on top of that. Then place the joker on top of the blacks. Place the other 13 reds on top of that, and finally place the remaining 13 blacks on top of that.

When ready to perform the trick for the spectator, turn the deck face up and fan the cards so that only you can see the faces. Remove the joker at the center and discard it. Split the deck at that point so that one group of 13 reds and 13 blacks is in each half of the deck.

Place the packets face down on the table. Instruct the spectator to riffle shuffle them together (as shown in Figure 17) and square up the pack. The shuffle should be fairly even for best results, so choose a spectator who can give the deck an even riffle shuffle.

After he has shuffled the cards, have him deal them into two even heaps. He is to deal from left to right, dealing a card alternately into each heap, until he has dealt all 52 cards.

Once he has done this, tell him to riffle shuffle the two heaps together again. At the conclusion of the second shuffle, take the deck from him and spread it so that you alone can see the cards. Remark that you are looking for some important cards. As you spread the cards from left to right you will note a large number of black cards at the bottom of the deck and a large number of red cards at the top of the deck. Depending on how even the shuffle was, there will be a few reds and a few blacks intermixed in the center of the deck.

Remove these intermixed cards and place them on the table. Cut or split the deck at the division between the colors so that reds are in one half, blacks in the other. Place each half face down on the table. Pick up the intermixed packet. Remove one red card and one black card. Remark that these cards have magical powers. Tap the red card against the top of the red packet. Pick up the red packet and spread it face up to show that all the cards are red. Pick up the black card, tap it against the black half, then spread that half to show that all the cards are black.

In many cases, if the shuffle is even, there will be no reds intermixed with blacks. In other words the colors will be perfectly separate at the conclusion of the second shuffle. In this case remove any red and any black. Cut the deck between the colors and proceed as described above.

To increase the chances for a perfect color separation, at the beginning stack the deck as follows from top down: 13 blacks, joker, 13 reds, 13 blacks, joker, 13 reds. Proceed with the trick as described above through the second riffle shuffle. When you then pick up the pack and look over the faces, you may find one or two cards intermixed at the center, but these are likely to be the jokers. Discard them from the deck. The colors should be perfectly separated at this point. If not, remove the few intermixed cards from the center and proceed as described above.

15 OIL AND WATER

The trick in which reds and blacks magically separate was noted as a card problem by the great nineteenth-century conjuror J. N. Hofzinser. A small-packet version was described by Walter Gibson in a magic magazine called *The Jinx.* Since its publication it has become a magic classic.

The effect is that four reds and four blacks are mixed together. Then they instantly separate. The simplest handling is described here.

Have four blacks in one pile and four reds in the other. Hold them as shown in Figure 10. Explain that there are numerous ways to mix reds and blacks, and that you will demonstrate one way.

The left thumb pushes over a red card so it drops face down onto the table. Then the right thumb pushes over a black card so it drops face down onto the table in a separate heap.

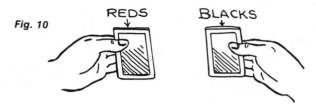

Fig. 10

The hands now cross, Figure 11. Thumb off a black card onto the tabled red card. At the same time the other hand thumbs off a red card onto the tabled black card.

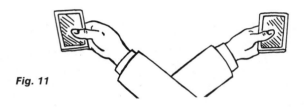

Fig. 11

Uncross the hands and thumb off another card from each packet onto the heaps that are on the table. Then cross the hands and thumb off the last card from each hand onto the tabled cards. You now have two packets on the table, each containing two reds and two blacks.

Pick up the left heap and place it on top of the right heap. Say, "That's how you mix the colors. It takes almost as long to unmix them." As you speak, deal the packet into two heaps, alternating a card to each, dealing from left to right. It appears as if you are separating the colors.

"Now I'll show you how magicians do it." Pick up the left heap and place it face down into the left hand. Pick up the other heap, turn it face up and place it into the right hand as in Figure 12. Turn the left hand palm down to show a black card at the bottom of the left hand heap. Turn the left hand palm up again, and turn the right hand palm down. Both packets are face down at this point.

Fig. 12

Thumb off the top card of the left-hand heap onto the table. Thumb off the *bottom* card of the right-hand heap onto the tabled card. Thumb off one more card from the top of the left-hand heap onto the tabled cards. Thumb off one more card from the bottom of the right-hand heap onto the tabled cards.

Then start a new packet on the table. Thumb off a card from each heap as before, alternating the cards, until you have dealt all four cards.

Snap your fingers over the first heap. Turn it face up and show that all cards are of one color. Turn over the other heap and show four cards of the opposite color. The colors have instantly separated.

16   CHECKERS

This is an offbeat version of "Oil and Water" devised by the author. Alternate three reds and three blacks, then hold the six-card packet face down in the left hand.

Turn the top card face up on top of the packet. Then deal the top two cards into a heap on the table. Pick them up as a unit, turn them over and replace them on top of the packet.

Deal the top three cards onto the table. Pick up the dealt packet, turn it over and replace it on top of the packet.

Deal the top four cards into a heap on the table. Pick up the dealt packet, turn it over and replace it on top of the packet.

Finally, deal the top five cards into a heap. Pick up the dealt cards, turn them over and replace them on top of the card in the left hand.

You will find that the colors still alternate but now every other card is reversed. If you do the trick without turning over the packet at each step the colors will separate. Deal smoothly and quickly to give the illusion that the cards are being completely mixed.

17   INFLUENTIAL PAIRS

Two cased decks are placed on the table. The spectator chooses either deck. This deck is thoroughly mixed by the spectator and the magician. The spectator then sorts these cards face up according to color. The magician follows suit with the other deck and matches the actions of the spectator but he does it with his cards face down.

Although the magician's cards are randomly dealt, when they are turned over it is seen that the colors have separated; all blacks are in one packet and all reds in another.

METHOD: This routine is based on ideas of Roy Walton and the author. Required are two decks, one red-backed and the other blue-backed. Stack the red deck so there are 26 pairs of cards such that each pair contains two cards of the same color. The actual order of the pairs is unimportant, although there should be a fair mixture of reds and blacks. Thus the red-backed deck might be stacked BB-BB-RR-BB-RR-BB-BB-RR-BB, and so on, from top to bottom.

The blue-backed deck is then stacked in exactly the same order. Once this has been done, deal the blue-backed deck onto the table a card at a time, thus reversing the order of the cards in this pack. Place each deck in its own card case until the time of performance.

To present the routine, toss out both cased decks. Ask the spectator to choose one pack. It can be either pack, but we'll assume he chooses the red deck. Remove it from its case and hand it to the spectator. Ask him to deal it into two heaps. He deals cards from right to left, a card at a time, until there are 26 cards in each heap.

Ask him to take either heap. You take the other one. Each of you places your half of the deck behind your back and mixes the cards. Actually you do nothing. Just place the packet behind your back and pretend to mix the cards.

Now the two halves of the red-backed deck are placed on the table alongside one another. Both halves are face down. The spectator removes a card from the tops of both heaps simultaneously. He turns them face up. If both are red they go into one packet on the table. If both are black they go into a separate packet. If one card is red and one is black they go into a discard packet off to one side.

As the spectator does this, you remove the blue-backed deck from its case and hold it in the left hand. Deal the top two cards off and take them with the right hand. Don't look at the faces of these two cards. Just follow the actions performed by the spectator. If he places his two cards into a face-up red pile, you place your two cards near his in a separate pile. If he then turns up two cards, sees they are black and puts them into a separate black pile, you take your next two cards from the blue-backed deck and place them in a pile near his black pile. If the spectator turns up two, sees that the colors don't match and places them in a discard pile, you place your pair of cards in a discard pile near his.

The spectator's pairs of cards will or won't match. The outcome is random on each round. You merely follow what he does but without looking at your cards. Yet although he has sorted match-ing-color pairs visibly, your pairs of cards sort themselves invisibly. At the finish of the deal, when you turn over your packet near his all-black packet, it will be seen that all of your cards are the same color. Similarly, when you turn over your packet near his all-red packet, all of the cards in your packet are seen to be of one color.

If the spectator wishes to examine your discard heap (the one next to his red-black heap), pick up the heap and transfer the top card to the bottom. Now all of the pairs in this heap will be nonmatching pairs.

18   RED MAGIC

Using his own deck of cards, which the magician has never seen before, the spectator removes any number of red cards and places these in his left jacket pocket. He then deals the remainder of the pack into two heaps, chooses either of these, sorts out the red cards in the chosen heap, and then places these in his right jacket pocket.

All of these actions take place while the magician has his back turned. Yet the magician now picks up the remaining heap on the table, glances briefly through it and immediately tells the spectator how many cards he has in *each* jacket pocket.

METHOD: Begin as described above by having the spectator re-move a number of red cards from the deck. Tell him to place them in his left jacket pocket. He must choose an even number for ease of working later on.

Now the spectator is directed to deal the remainder of the deck into two heaps, each heap containing the same number of cards. After the deal he can shuffle each heap.

He then chooses either heap, sorts out all the red cards and places them in his right jacket pocket. The magician picks up the remain-ing heap and mentally counts the number of reds and the number of blacks in it.

A quick mental calculation is performed as follows. To the num-ber of red cards in this heap the magician adds *twice* the number of black cards and from the result subtracts 26. The number arrived at is the number of red cards in the spectator's right jacket pocket.

As an example, if the heap examined by the magician contains ten reds and 12 blacks, he would add 10 + 24, getting 34. From this he subtracts 26, getting 8. This tells him that the spectator has eight red cards in his right jacket pocket.

You have accounted for eight reds in the spectator's right pocket and ten reds in the packet you examined. Since the pack contains 26 red cards in all, the spectator must have eight reds in his left jacket pocket.

19   ODD COLOR OUT

A packet of cards is removed from the deck and handed to a spectator sitting across the table from you. He places the cards below the level of the tabletop, cuts them and completes the cut. Then he turns the top two cards face up, places them on top of the face-down packet and cuts the packet. He turns two more cards face up, places them on top of the packet and again cuts and completes the cut. The process continues as long as the spectator desires. Each time he turns over the top two cards, places them on top of the packet and cuts the packet. The result will be a random distribution of face-up and face-down cards in the packet.

When the spectator is satisfied that face-up and face-down cards are hopelessly mixed, tell him to glance at the top card of the packet and the bottom card. If these are of different colors, he remembers each card, turns each over, then returns each to its original position. Then he cuts the packet to lose these two cards. If the top and bottom cards are of the same color, he cuts the packet until he brings a card of each color to top and bottom of the packet.

With the two noted cards buried in the packet, the cards are handed to the magician under the table. He sorts through the cards briefly, then brings the packet into view and spreads it out on the table to reveal a surprising outcome. All of the face-up cards are red except for the previously noted *black* card. The packet is flipped over to reveal that all of the face-up cards now in view are black except for the previously noted *red* card!

METHOD: This excellent close-up mystery is based on ideas of Bob Hummer and Robert Page. You will need a stack of about 20 cards. The colors alternate red-black-red-black from top to bottom. This is the only preparation.

When ready to present the trick, hand this packet to the spectator. He places it below the level of the tabletop, cuts the packet and completes the cut. The trick then proceeds exactly as described above. When the spectator pushes over the top two cards and reverses them, he must reverse them as a unit. This is to say that the top two cards are pushed over, taken with the right hand, turned over and replaced on top of the packet.

After the spectator has noted the top and bottom card and reversed each in place, he cuts the packet and completes the cut. The position of the two chosen cards is not known to anyone, nor is the order of face-up and face-down cards in the packet. The packet is handed to you under the table or behind your back. All you need do is reverse every other card. Then bring the packet into view and spread it on the table. All of the face-up cards will be red except for the previously noted black card. When the packet is flipped over, all of the face-up cards will be black except for the previously noted red card.

Performed seemingly on the spur of the moment with an unprepared deck of cards, this is an all but unfathomable mystery. There is another way to go directly into the trick using a shuffled deck of cards, but it is not impromptu. The idea is to have a packet of 20 cards on the lap already set up as described above. After doing a few card tricks with the deck on the table, cut off about 20 cards and have the spectator shuffle the packet. Take back the packet and give it another shuffle. Then hand it to the spectator under the table. Actually, when the packet goes under the table, switch it for the duplicate packet in the lap. Since this packet is stacked in the correct order with the colors alternating, the trick works exactly as described. You will have to put the cards away after the routine is done because the cards in this packet won't necessarily match the cards in the packet you cut off the deck, but you may find the effect worth the extra effort.

20 THE COLOR OF THOUGHT

In *Self-Working Card Tricks* a routine called "Opposites Attract" introduced a novel method of making kings and queens match. Here, in the closing routine of this chapter, Martin Gardner provides an ingenious application in which the spectator correctly guesses the color of every card in the pack!

Set up the deck so that all the reds are in the top half and all the blacks in the bottom half. Spread the deck face down on the table. Invite the spectator to push 26 cards out partially from the spread. Be sure to keep mental count of the number of cards he pushes out so you can stop him at 26. The situation might look like Figure 13 at this point.

Mention that, to make sure he has exactly 26 cards, you will count them. Take each card he pushed out, beginning at the top (or

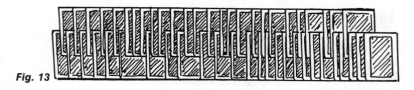

Fig. 13

right-hand end) of the spread, and deal or place them into a pile, counting aloud as you take each card. This procedure secretly reverses the cards. Make sure the cards stay in order.

Square up the remainder of the spread. Pick up this packet. Tell the spectator you want to make a quick check of the count. Turn the packet so you alone can see the faces and fan them toward you. Pretend to make a quick count. Actually you spot the reds remaining in the top half and note the last card of this run. Say the last red card is the ♦7.

Place the two packets alongside each other. Say, "It seems you did rather well. Look." Deal cards simultaneously from the tops of both packets. In Figure 14 the packets are placed at *A* and *B*. You deal cards off the tops of the packets, turn them face up and place them in face-up packets *C* and *D* as shown in Figure 14. Continue dealing until your previously noted key card (the ♦7 in our example) turns up.

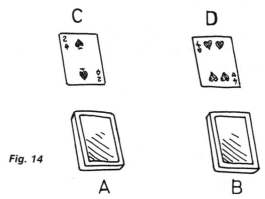

Fig. 14

By this time the audience assumes the entire deck has been correctly separated into reds and blacks by the spectator. As if in recognition of this, say, "Let's not waste time turning up single cards."

Pick up the packet at *D* and spread it at a spot above the layout.

Then spread C below it. The situation as it now looks is shown in Figure 15.

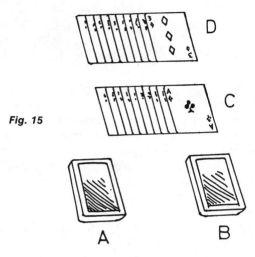

Fig. 15

A subtlety in the handling comes into play at this point. Pick up the packet at A, turn it face up and spread it as a continuation of the spread at D. The audience sees all cards of one color.

Finish by picking up the pile at B, turning it face up and spreading it as a continuation of the spread at C. All cards show the other color.

This is a simple, natural handling of an extremely strong card routine. In effect the spectator has correctly guessed the color of every card in the deck.

TELEPHONE TRICKS

In the early part of this century a new effect was introduced, based on the remarkable premise that it was possible to perform mind reading over the telephone. Since its inception, the telephone trick has inspired many variations and developments. Some of the best are described in this chapter.

21 TWENTIETH-CENTURY TELEPATHY

This is the original telephone trick, devised by John N. Hilliard and published in 1905. With attention to dramatic presentation, it is still one of the best demonstrations of telephone telepathy. The details of performance are important. Hilliard urged that the trick be done as an experiment in long-distance telepathy rather than as a card trick. The following description is taken from his original article.

Have someone go into the next room. Explain that this person will be a committee of one, delegated to call the medium at a later time. When he is out of the room, tell one of the spectators that you would like him to name a card. It can be any card in the deck but to make the demonstration meaningful the spectator should try not to name an obvious card.

We will assume the ♣K is named. The spectator in the next room is called back. He acknowledges that he is not a confederate and that he has no idea which card was chosen. He is given the name and telephone number of the medium. He dials the number and asks the medium to call out the name of the thought-of card. Immediately she names the exact card merely thought of by the spectator!

The magician never leaves the room and does not communicate

with the medium. The spectator may think of any card in the deck. There is no force and there is no confederacy involved. Properly performed it is an astounding trick.

METHOD: In a sense the method has been included in the above description of the effect but it seems such an incidental detail that the reader is likely to have overlooked it. The secret is that when you convey the medium's name to the spectator you have furnished a code which transmits the name of the chosen card to the medium. To say it another way, you choose one of 52 names for the medium and that name tells her the chosen card.

On a card write down the following information:

	Hearts	*Clubs*	*Diamonds*	*Spades*
Ace	Sidney	Dobson	Colt	Harris
Two	Smith	Darrow	Carver	Holmes
Three	Schmidt	Driscoll	Campbell	Hart
Four	Sanford	Dwight	Christopher	Hanford
Five	Scofield	Drew	Cartwright	Hamlin
Six	Stoddard	Draper	Caldwell	Haskins
Seven	Samson	Dayton	Cortland	Herne
Eight	Saddler	Dodge	Craig	Hicks
Nine	Seager	Davis	Cabot	Hoffman
Ten	Snyder	Drake	Case	Holt
Jack	Scranton	Dawson	Clark	Higgins
Queen	Sarles	Denton	Collins	Hodges
King	Spencer	Daley	Curtis	Hartz

On the back of this card write the medium's telephone number. The medium has a duplicate of this list of names which she keeps near the telephone.

Proceed as described above to have the volunteer spectator leave the room while you have a card named. As soon as the card is named, have the volunteer return to the room. Take the above card out of your pocket with the name side toward you. If the named card is the ♥A for example, have the spectator dial the number and ask for Mrs. Sidney. If the named card is the ♦6, have the volunteer ask for Mrs. Caldwell. In our example the named card is the ♣K. Here you would have the volunteer go to the phone, dial the number and ask for Mrs. Daley.

On her end of the phone the medium consults her list and sees that Mrs. Daley is the code for the ♣K. She then goes on with a dramatic revelation of this card.

In the original article Hilliard concluded with these wise words: "If worked in a dramatic manner, a single trial will convince the most skeptical that the experiment has a remarkable and totally inexplicable effect on an audience."

22 THE PERCIVAL CODE

In the original article Hilliard suggested an alternate code that is somewhat more brief. This code assigns letters of the alphabet to the values of the cards and letters to the suits. The letters A through M are assigned to the values ace through king, and the letters D, I, T, E to the suits clubs, hearts, spades and diamonds respectively.

Using this code, if the spectator chose the ♥A, the volunteer would be instructed to dial the phone and ask for Mrs. A. I. Smith. If the spectator chose the ♣6, the volunteer would ask for Mrs. F. D. Smith, and so on.

Another approach is this. Use Hilliard's Sidney through Spencer column to code values, and the following code for suits:

Alice	= clubs	Carol	= spades
Betty	= hearts	Ethel	= diamonds

If the spectator names the ♣A, the volunteer is to ask for Alice Sidney. If he named the ♦A, the volunteer would ask for Ethel Sidney. If the named card was the ♠J, the volunteer would ask for Carol Scranton, and so on. Thus the medium's first name codes the suit of the named card, while her last name codes the value. This cuts down on the size of the list and makes it easier to find the proper name. The method is related to one published by John Percival.

Still another method is to assign a different card to each week of the year. Since there are 52 weeks in the year and 52 cards in the deck, each card can be associated with a particular week. The medium keeps a calendar near the phone, looks up the card for the current week, and knows which card to name when asked. But note that although no code is used in this version, it is necessary to force the card for that particular week. The chapter on forces later in this book provides information on forcing any card you desire. In this version of the telephone trick the spectator cannot name any card in the deck, but the fact that no code is used might make this approach appealing to the reader.

23 CALLING MS. WIZARD

In this version of the telephone trick the medium's name and phone number are known from the start, yet she is able to name any thought-of card. The idea is this. Have someone name any card. You then go to the phone and dial the medium's number. When she picks up the phone she begins counting from one to 13. When she calls out the value of the named card, you say, "Hello?"

If for example she called out, "One, two, three, four——" and you said, "Hello?" she would know that the value of the thought-of card was four because you said "hello" immediately after the medium said "four."

As soon as she knows the value, the medium calls out the suits. When she calls out the suit of the thought-of card, you say, "Hello?" once again. For example, if she called out, "Clubs, spades——" and you said "Hello?" she would know that the suit is spades, because you said "hello" right after she called out spades.

Immediately hand the phone to the spectator. He asks the medium to name the chosen card. Since she now knows the suit and value, she can go on to reveal the card in dramatic fashion.

This trick once sold for a considerable sum. One of the simplest and best methods of transmitting any card in the deck to the medium without the use of a name code, it is credited to Bill McCaffrey.

24 THE GREAT PHONE MYSTERY

The spectator is given the deck behind his back. He removes the top card, turns it over and inserts it anywhere in the deck. Then he removes the bottom card, turns it over and inserts it anywhere in the pack.

Spreading the pack face down on the table, he finds the first reversed card and the card that is face to face with it. Then he finds the other reversed card and removes the card that is face to face with it.

There are now two random cards on the table. The spectator goes to the phone, dials the medium and calls out one of the two random cards. The medium immediately names the *other* random card!

There is no code. The spectator handles the cards from start to finish. He can know the medium's name and phone number ahead of time.

METHOD: This approach introduces the idea of a force. Beforehand you and the medium agree on a card that will be forced. Say
it is the ♥9. Place the ♥9 near the bottom of the deck. Then place
a card face up under it so the reversed card is face to face with the
♥9. Then reverse the bottom card. The prepared deck is shown in
Figure 16. The ♦2 and ♣3 are face up in the drawing.

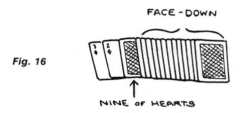

Fig. 16

FACE - DOWN

NINE OF HEARTS

To present the trick remove the deck from its case. Holding it
face down, hand it to the spectator behind his back. Tell him to
take the top card, turn it over and insert it anywhere in the pack.
Then tell him to take the bottom card, turn it over and insert it
somewhere else in the pack. Finally ask him to cut the deck and
complete the cut.

He brings the deck into view and spreads it face down on the
table. There will be two face-up cards in the pack. Have the spectator remove the card that is face to face with each of the reversed
cards. Caution him not to turn either of these cards face up.

Since you knew at the start which card was facing the ♥9, you
know which of the two cards on the table must be the ♥9. Have
the spectator turn the other card face up. He dials the medium and
names this card. She then reveals the identity of the other card, the
♥9.

25 A REMOTE MIRACLE

As this routine illustrates, the telephone trick has developed in
an unexpected direction. In this version you do not call the medium. Instead you call a friend and perform the entire trick for him
over the telephone, as follows:

Using his own shuffled deck, the spectator deals out two poker
hands of five cards each. He chooses one hand, shuffles it and notes
the top card. Then he takes a few cards from the top of the deck

and places them on this hand to bury the chosen card. The deck is then dropped onto the hand containing the chosen card. Finally the deck is dropped onto the other poker hand. The spectator calls off the cards in order from the top of the deck. When he has called off all the cards, the magician on the other end of the line immediately names the chosen card.

METHOD: All of the above is intended to make the trick appear more sophisticated than it really is. What the method comes down to is this: the chosen card will always be tenth up from the bottom of the deck, or forty-third down from the top. All you need to do is call a friend, have him follow the above instructions, then simply note the forty-third card he calls out. That will be the chosen card.

26 POKER BY PHONE

In this novel routine the magician remarks that he has a friend who can play Stud Poker by telephone. The spectator freely chooses a card. There is no force. The spectator signs his name on the card. Then he adds four more cards to it to make a Five-Card Stud Poker hand. He mixes the five cards and turns one of them face down for the hole card. Then he calls off the four face-up cards to the medium over the telephone.

Without asking a question she names the hole card, then she goes on to name the card signed by the spectator!

The spectator may call out the four face-up cards in any order. There is no code. The medium's name and phone number are known to the spectator ahead of time. The spectator has a free choice of cards, and the name of his card need not be known to the magician.

METHOD: The trick uses a force but the subtle angle is that the card chosen by the spectator is not the force card. In fact it is the only card that is not forced.

On top of the deck have four known cards. Say they are the ♣A, ♥4, ♠8 and ♦J. This is the only preparation. These four cards must be known to the medium ahead of time. She can jot them down on a slip of paper and have the paper near the phone in readiness for this trick.

When ready to present the routine, place the deck face down on the table. Ask the spectator to cut off about half and place it on the table. Then hand him the lower half, and ask him to shuffle it and place it on top of the tabled half, but at right angles. A view of the situation at this point is shown in Figure 46 on page 78.

Remove a slip of paper from the pocket. Written on it is the name and phone number of the medium. Place it in full view on the table. Then have the spectator take the top card of the top packet, look at it and sign his name across the face.

Lift off the upper packet and place it aside. Then deal the top four cards of the lower packet onto the table. These are the four cards you placed on top of the deck previously, but it looks as if they are four random cards from the middle of the pack.

Have the spectator add his signed card to the four dealt cards. Then tell him to mix them face up and turn one face down. If it is the signed card, have him turn three more cards face down so that only one card remains face up. Tell him this will be the hole card. The hole card must not be the signed card, but it can be any other card.

The situation now is that there are four face-up cards on the table and one face-down card. Remark that this represents a Stud Poker hand and that the medium has the ability to play Stud Poker by phone.

The spectator calls the medium and names the four face-up cards in any order. Knowing what the four force cards are, the medium notes which one was *not* called out. This is the hole card. If for example the spectator calls out ♣A, ♥4, ♠8 and ♣3, the medium notes that the ♦J was not called out so she knows this must be the hole card. Further, the spectator called out the ♣3, which is not one of the four cards on her list, so she knows this must be the signed card. She then goes on to reveal the identity of the hole card and the signed card.

In keeping with the poker theme, instead of having the spectator sign the face of his card, have him place an X on the back. Explain that this card represents a marked card since it is marked on the back. You further explain that you know someone who can play Stud Poker over the telephone and who has the remarkable ability of being able to detect marked cards via telephone. The medium is called, she names the hole card, then ponders a bit and goes on to identify the marked card.

27   SHYLOCK'S CARD

Whereas Sherlock Holmes always caught the guilty man by brilliant deduction, his infamous brother Shylock Holmes always sent the innocent man to the electric chair. The ♥J is used in this trick to represent Shylock, and the entire detective story is enacted over the phone.

1. Call a friend and have him bring a deck of cards to the phone. When he has done this, ask him to remove the ♥J and place it aside for the moment.

2. Tell him to remove three kings, say the ♥K, ♠K and ♦K, from the deck and arrange them in that order in a face-up row on the table.

3. The spectator mentally decides which king is to be the guilty party. He signifies this by placing the Shylock card (♥J) face up under the chosen king.

4. Then he turns the chosen king face down so that the king is face-to-face with Shylock. "Shylock gets an excellent look at the killer. In fact he can't get a better look. But you can bet he'll disgrace himself by picking the wrong man later on."

5. Ask the spectator to exchange the guilty party with one of the other kings. Then he exchanges the face-down king with the other face-up king.

6. This step is optional. Have him exchange the two face-up cards and call out their positions. Then have him exchange these two cards again. (The spectator, in calling out the positions of these two kings, need only say whether each is on the left, in the middle or on the right. Then have him exchange these two cards again.)

7. Have the spectator turn the two face-up kings face down. Say, "Shylock is face-to-face with one of the suspects. Since he's positive this fellow is the guilty man, we know he's wrong. Place this king back in the deck."

8. There are two kings left on the table. To name the guilty party you use the information of Step 6. If the spectator called out positions 1 and 2, you know the guilty party is not the king originally in position 3. That is, the guilty party is not the king in the position that was not called on. Since the kings were originally in heart-spade-diamond order in Step 2, you know the guilty party is not the ♦K. Have the spectator discard this king. The remaining king on the table is the guilty party.

If the spectator called out positions 1 and 3, the ♠K would not be guilty. If the spectator called out positions 2 and 3, the ♥K would not be the guilty party. Thus, whatever positions the spectator calls out in Step 6, you know who is not guilty.

As mentioned, Step 6 is optional. Instead of having the spectator exchange the two face-up cards and then exchange them again, you can have him simply call out the positions of the two face-up kings. The rest of the trick is as written.

This routine is the author's version of a principle suggested by Bob Hummer. A remarkable version of Hummer's idea is the routine that closes this chapter.

28 NO QUESTIONS ASKED

This clever version of the telephone trick was marketed by Richard Himber. Call a friend and tell him to take his own cards, shuffle them and deal out two heaps. He is to deal from left to right and he can stop whenever he likes, as long as there are the same number of cards in both heaps.

After he has done this, tell him to place the undealt portion of the deck in his pocket. Then tell him to lift up a portion of cards from the left-hand heap and note the bottom or face card of the cut portion. He then places this portion on the right-hand heap.

There will be some cards remaining in the left-hand heap. Have him call them off to you over the phone. When he's done this, say, "Your card is the —— Wait, I forgot, your card is in the *other* heap. All right, call out the cards in the right-hand heap."

He does this and you immediately name the chosen card.

The secret is this. When he calls out the cards in the small left-hand packet, list them on a piece of paper, one under the other. When he calls out the cards in the large right-hand heap, list them under the other cards you've written down.

You may have a total of 20 cards. Half of 20 is ten. The tenth card he called out is his chosen card. The chosen card is always at a position that is half the total number of cards. If, for example, he called out 24 cards, his card would be the twelfth card he called out.

As soon as you name the card, hang up. Chances are excellent the spectator will call you back and ask how you did it!

29 THE CONNECTION

Most of the tricks in this book require nothing in the way of special apparatus. This routine is an exception, although the apparatus is something you are likely to own. The gimmick makes possible miracle tricks like the following.

While at a friend's home ask him to remove a deck of cards from its case, spread the cards face up on the table and remove any card. He can change his mind as often as he likes until he finally decides on one card.

You then dial the medium's number but hand the phone directly to the spectator while the phone on the other end is still ringing. The medium picks up the phone and instantly announces the name of the chosen card!

There is no code and the effect may be repeated immediately. The medium can be in the next town or across the country. The spectator has an absolutely free choice of any card in the deck. He can even make up the name of a card, like the twenty of clubs, or he can think of some other object like a key or a picture or a coin. If he thinks of the title of a tune, the medium will pick up the phone on her end and immediately whistle the tune. Before proceeding you may wish to try to figure out a method that will answer the above conditions.

METHOD: The special apparatus mentioned above is a cassette tape recorder. All you do is have someone dial your phone, turn on the tape recorder and record the ringing phone. Then record the sound made when you pick up the phone. That completes the preparation. Rewind the tape, place it next to the phone, have your medium ready, and you can now perform a perplexing mystery.

When at the home of a friend, have him choose a card as outlined above. Make sure he has time to change his mind so that he won't think he merely picked an obvious card. When he has a card in mind, go to the phone and dial the medium.

As soon as the phone rings, she takes it off the hook and starts the tape recorder. Hand the phone to the spectator. He hears the sound of a ringing phone and thinks it is the medium's phone that's ringing. Actually it's only a *recording* of a ringing phone, but he doesn't know that.

Say to him, "Now remember to get a clear mental picture of the four of clubs" (or whatever card he chose). When you name the card to him, the medium on the other end of the line hears your remarks and thus knows the card.

The phone rings four or five more times. Then there is the recorded sound of the phone being picked up. The medium now comes on the line and merely names the card she just heard you mention. Properly built up, this is a trick of sensational impact.

30   LINEAR BLACKJACK

This is the game of blackjack played over the telephone. Though you never see the cards, never touch them and never ask a single question, you always win at this game.

Call a friend and have him bring a deck of cards to the phone. Tell him you and he are going to play a little game of blackjack. He is to deal a jack to himself and a jack to you. These represent the hole cards.

Then have him remove any ace, two and three from the deck. He is to place them in a row in any order. You do not know the order. Tell him to exchange the three with the card to the right of it. If there is no card to the right of the three, he does nothing.

Then have him exchange the ace with the card to the left of it. If there is no card to the left of the ace, he does nothing.

Finally have him exchange the two with the card to the right of it. If there is no card to the right of the two, he does nothing.

Remind the spectator that he dealt the three cards out in any order and that you had him mix them without your knowing which card was where. Now you will pick one of the three cards to go with your jack. Tell him you want the card on the far left. It will be the ace. If he takes either the two or the three, or even if he takes both the two and the three for himself, he cannot beat your score of 21.

METHOD: In the above trick, devised by the author, you need simply follow the instructions as given. The three cards can be in any order at the start. The spectator tells you nothing. Have him move the cards around as described, then tell him you want the card on the left. It will always be the ace.

31   THE ULTRA CODE

The spectator chooses any one of the four suits, then removes any five cards in that suit to form a poker hand. The magician gives him the name and phone number of the medium. He explains that he wants the spectator to choose one of the five cards and turn it face down. Then he is to read off the other four cards to the medium over the phone. He can read the cards in any order.

When he has done this the medium instantly names the value and suit of the face-down card.

This routine is somewhat similar to "Poker By Phone" (No. 26) but here there is no force. The spectator can choose any five cards. Since the method is completely different, it forms an ideal follow-up trick.

METHOD: This is the author's solution to a stud-poker problem proposed by Fitch Cheney. The curious feature of this approach is that although a code is used, the code is determined *before* the spectator chooses a card.

Have the spectator name one of the four suits. Then tell him to remove any five cards in that suit. Explain that you are going to try to transmit telepathic impressions of these cards and, to make it easier, the spectator should select spot cards rather than picture cards.

As he removes five cards from the face-up deck, mentally add together their values. If for example he removes the ♣5, ♣3, ♣7, ♣8 and ♣2, you would silently add together 5 + 3 + 7 + 8 + 2, arriving at a total of 25. You now remove a small book from your pocket, apparently to get the medium's telephone number. One page of the book contains the following information:

TOTAL	NAME	TOTAL	NAME	
15	Abbott	28	Hardin	
16	Thompson	29	Jaks	
17	Ashworth	30	Jordan	Clubs = Alice
18	Baker	31	Rodgers	
19	Buckley	32	Lyons	Hearts = Betty
20	Collins	33	Rawson	
21	Dalton	34	Stanyon	Spades = Carol
22	Davenport	35	Tarbell	
23	Downs	36	Walsh	Diamonds = Jean
24	Ducrot	37	Taylor	
25	Elliott	38	Nielsen	
26	Gardner	39	Simpson	
27	Horowitz	40	Palmer	

Since you know the total of the five cards, look up that figure and note the name opposite it. In our example the total is 25. The name opposite 25 is Elliott. This means that you will tell the spectator that the medium's last name is Elliott.

In our example the spectator selected clubs for the suit. Since the suit is clubs, you will tell the spectator that the medium's first name is Alice.

Jot down this information on a blank page of the book, write in the medium's phone number, tear out the page and hand it to the spectator. In our example he will be directed to phone the number you gave him and ask for Alice Elliott.

Close the book and put it away. There should be no suspicion attached to the book because the spectator has not yet chosen a card. Ask him to look over the five cards and choose one. He is to signal his choice by turning the chosen card face down. Have him go to the phone and dial the number you gave him.

When he asks for Alice Elliott, the medium knows that the suit is clubs (because Alice = clubs) and she knows that the total of all five cards is 25 (because Elliott = 25).

Now the spectator reads off the four remaining cards in any order. The medium jots down their values, totals the four numbers and subtracts this total from 25. Whatever the result, that is the value of the chosen card. If, say, the spectator called out 8, 2, 3, 5, the medium would note that the total is 18. Subtracting 18 from 25, she gets an answer of 7. Thus she knows that the chosen card is the ♣7.

To take another example, suppose the spectator dials the medium's number and asks for Jean Baker. The medium knows that the suit is diamonds (because Jean = diamonds) and that the total of all five cards is 18 (because Baker = 18). If the spectator then reads off four cards and they total 12, the medium would announce that the chosen card is the ♦6.

The trick can be done with any five random cards taken from the full deck of 52 cards. In this case suits would have to be given numerical values and summed the same way that values are handled. The details are left to the interested reader.

32 TIME SQUARED

We close this chapter with an outstanding telephone mystery. Calling the spectator on the phone, the mentalist asks him to note the time on his watch, and to remove three cards from the deck corresponding to that time. If, for example, the spectator's watch indicated it was 8:53, the spectator would remove an eight, a five and a three from the deck. He arranges them in a row on the table to indicate the correct time.

Remarking on the well-known phrase that time is money, the

magician tells the spectator to place a quarter on any card. He is then to exchange the other two cards. After the exchange there will be a new time indicated by the three cards. The spectator calls out this new time, whereupon the magician instantly reveals on which card the spectator placed the coin.

METHOD: This trick is the diabolical invention of Fr. Cyprian. Note that because the time on the spectator's watch is different from the time on your watch, you could not know which three cards he removed from the deck. Since you do not know the three cards, it is impossible to have enough information to conclude the trick without asking questions.

But in fact you do know something about the time on the spectator's watch. While it is true you do not know the exact setting, you know exactly where the hour hand points. Thus if your watch indicates 8:51, his watch might indicate 8:52 or 8:57 or 8:49. In each case the first digit is an 8, and it is on this subtle point that the ingenious method depends. When the spectator places three cards on the table to indicate the time on his watch, you know that the card on the left will be an 8.

The rest of the method derives from a Hummer principle. Have the spectator remove the three cards and place them in a row to indicate the time. Then tell him to place a coin on one card. When he has done this, have him exchange the other two cards. Then have him call out the new time to you.

In our example you call the spectator sometime between eight and nine o'clock so the first card on the left should be an eight. If it is an eight when he calls out the time, then the coin is on the eight. If the eight is in the middle, the coin rests on the rightmost card. If the eight is on the right end, the coin is on the middle card.

There is one final point. Do the trick between one o'clock and ten o'clock. This avoids the confusion of having to use picture cards to represent later hours.

RIFFLE-SHUFFLE SETUPS

Riffle-shuffle setups represent one of the newest areas to emerge in card magic. In tricks of this nature the spectator is allowed to shuffle the deck. Although it would seem that the deck is in random order after the shuffle, in fact the magician can control the distribution of cards in the entire deck. It is this surprising fact which leads to strong card tricks using shuffle setups.

Except where noted, the material in this chapter is from my own files. The chapter begins with simple ideas and then goes on to more sophisticated tricks using riffle-shuffle setups. Occasionally familiar plot ideas are employed but they emerge here in unexpected new ways.

Tricks using riffle-shuffle setups exploit a kind of thinking that is different from anything else in card magic. It is not unlikely to find that although you know how these tricks work, you are not sure why. This chapter represents a roundup of current thinking in a provocative area of card magic.

33 STACK A PACK

One of the basic principles of riffle-shuffle setups has to do with a method of controlling the distribution of colors. The idea is that the spectator shuffles the deck, but despite this, you know how the colors are distributed throughout. The following idea is too simple to fool anyone, but it will quickly and easily illustrate the basic method.

Two packets are used. One contains a red card on top followed by a black card. The other packet contains a black card on top followed by a red card. Place the two-card packets side by side. Riffle shuffle them together as shown in Figure 17, and square up the cards. Deal off the top two cards. You will find that one of these cards is black and the other is red. Look at the remaining two cards and you will see exactly the same situation; one of these cards is black and the other is red.

Fig. 17

This simple stunt represents a basic principle of riffle-shuffle setups, for it is true that no matter how unevenly the two packets are shuffled together you will *always* end up with a red and a black among the top two cards, and a red and black among the bottom two cards. No other result is possible. This idea is exploited in the following trick.

34 MAGNETIC COLORS

The spectator gives the deck a riffle shuffle. Although the shuffle appears to be completely random, the spectator finds on dealing off pairs of cards that *every* pair contains exactly one red and one black card!

METHOD: This routine was independently devised by Gene Finnell, Norman Gilbreath and others. Preparation consists of arranging the deck so that the colors alternate red-black-red-black from top to bottom.

Cut the deck at about the midpoint. The only stipulation is that there is a red card on the bottom of one half and a black card on the bottom of the other half. Place the two packets side by side. Tell the spectator you are going to control the way he shuffles the deck even though you will not touch the cards.

The spectator gives the deck one riffle shuffle. He then deals pairs of cards off the top and turns each pair face up. He should be surprised to discover that each pair contains one red card and one black card.

Laymen think that a riffle shuffle destroys any possible order of the cards. They are therefore baffled to discover that even though they shuffled the deck, the cards are still in order!

35 SELF-MATCHING COLORS

It is possible to alter the basic setup so that colors match up. You cannot say when a pair of the same color will show up but you can definitely say what the matching colors will be.

Arrange ten cards so the colors alternate red-black-red-black and so on. Then arrange another ten-card packet in identically the same order. Riffle shuffle the two packets together.

Deal a pair of cards off the top. It may contain two cards of the same color. If so, that color will be red. If the pair contains one red and one black, toss it aside. Deal off the next pair. If the first pair didn't match but the second did, then this pair will contain two reds. In other words, the first matching pair to turn up, even if it's the fifth pair you deal, will contain two red cards.

The next matching pair you turn up, whether it's the next pair or the last pair, will contain two black cards. You can't say when this new pair of matching colors will turn up, but you can say with certainty what colors it will contain.

Matching-color pairs will alternate throughout the shuffled packet. In other words, the first matching-color pair will contain two reds. The next matching-color pair will contain two blacks. The next matching-color pair (if there is one) must contain two reds. The next must contain two blacks, and so on. Of course there will be times when the packet will contain no matching-color pairs. But if there are pairs containing two cards of the same color, you can say positively what those colors will be.

36 A DEVILISH SECRET

Red and black cards seem to attract one another in strange ways. To illustrate, the magician has the spectator give the deck a riffle shuffle and begin turning pairs of cards face up, beginning at the top of the pack. When a pair of black cards is turned up, the magician states that the next pair of cards will be red. The spectator turns up the next pair and these cards are indeed red.

Continuing to deal pairs of cards, the spectator finds that every time he deals a matching pair of one color, the very next pair of cards will match and will be of the opposite color.

METHOD: The deck is stacked. The arrangement from the top down is red-black-black-red, red-black-black-red, and so on, this same sequence repeating through the pack.

To present the trick, cut the deck approximately at its midpoint, between two red cards. Place the two packets in front of the spectator. Invite him to riffle shuffle them together. After the shuffle he deals pairs of cards off the top. Whenever a matching pair is dealt, the next matching pair will be of the opposite color.

37   ESP + MATH

The spectator shuffles two packets of cards together. Then he deals off the top three cards and hands them to the magician behind his back. If the packet contains at least two cards of the same suit, the magician reveals the matching suit. Then, with the packet still behind his back, he finds at least one of the matching-suit cards.

The process is repeated until there are no cards left. Each time the magician correctly reveals the matching suit and then goes on to find one card of that suit, always with the cards behind his back.

METHOD: This trick introduces a different idea in riffle-shuffle setups. Here you not only know *which* cards will match, you know *where* one of them will be, even though the cards have been shuffled by the spectator.

Stack one 12-card packet spades-diamonds-hearts, this same sequence repeated throughout the packet. Then stack another 12-card packet spades-hearts-diamonds, this same sequence repeated throughout the packet.

When ready to present the trick, hand the two packets to the spectator. Have him riffle shuffle them together. Turn your back. Tell him to deal the top three cards into a heap. Then have him pick up this three-card packet, turn it face up and note if it contains at least two cards of the same suit.

If it does, he hands you the packet behind your back. The first packet of matching-suit cards will contain two spades and, further, at least one spade will be at the bottom or face of the packet. When the packet is handed to you behind your back, pretend to concentrate, then reveal that the matching suits are spades. Pause, then say that you will try to find one of the matching spade cards by sense of touch.

Act as if great powers of concentration are required, but all you need do is remove the bottom card of the packet and bring it into view. Show that you were correct in finding one of the matching spades.

Bring the remainder of the packet out from behind your back. Toss the three cards face up onto the table. Simply note which suit is *not* represented among the three cards. This will be the matching suit in the next group of cards the spectator gives you. Assume the missing suit is diamonds.

The spectator deals off the next three cards into a face-down heap. While you turn your back, he notes if this packet contains at least two cards of the same suit. If it does, he hands it to you behind your back. If it doesn't, he discards it and deals three more cards. He continues to deal three-card packets until he finds one which contains at least two cards of the same suit. Then he hands you this packet behind your back.

In our example, when the spectator hands you the next matching pair packet behind your back, you reveal that the matching suit is diamonds. Then remove the bottom card and bring it into view to show that you have located one card of the matching suit. Continue in this way until all of the cards have been handed to you. With no change in handling you can have each three-card packet placed in an envelope and handed to you behind your back. You reveal the matching suit, then reach into the envelope and remove a card of the matching suit. The use of envelopes seems to isolate the cards, making the effect more difficult. Actually the envelopes do not affect the handling in any way.

38   COLOR PROPHECY

In this puzzling effect, devised by Gene Finnell, the spectator shuffles the pack and deals it into two heaps. He takes either heap and gives the other to the performer.

The performer runs through his cards and openly turns several of them face up. Then he places the heap on the table. The performer explains that he has made an odd sort of prediction with his cards. He and the spectator will deal cards simultaneously from the tops of the heaps. If the performer deals a face-down card, it will not match the color of the card dealt by the spectator. But when the performer deals a face-up card, it will match the color of the card dealt by the spectator.

The dealing commences and each time the performer deals a face-up card, it does in fact match the color of the spectator's card.

METHOD: Arrange the pack so that the colors alternate red-black-red-black throughout. Cut the deck so there is a red card at the face of one packet and a black card at the face of the other. Have the spectator riffle shuffle the two halves together and then deal the deck into two equal heaps, alternating a card into each heap as he deals.

Pick up either heap and run through it two cards at a time. Examine each pair. If the pair contains a red and black card, turn this pair over as a single card. Thus, if the rightmost card of the pair was red, then after the pair is turned over the red card will be on the left. It is important to turn over each pair separately, one pair at a time as you go through the packet.

At the completion of this process you'll have several face-up cards in the packet. Place the packet on the table. Then cards are dealt simultaneously off the top of both heaps. If the performer deals a face-down card, the pair will be a mismatch, that is, one red card and one black. But if the performer deals a face-up card, the spectator will deal a card of the same color.

The trick is automatic and never fails to impress the onlooker since he shuffled the cards at the very beginning of the trick.

39 BLIND CHOICE

This brilliant trick, invented by Roy Walton, is one in which both the spectator and the performer successfully guess the colors of the cards. The routine has not previously appeared in print.

Stack the deck so the colors alternate red-black-red-black from top to bottom. Hand the pack to a spectator and have him cut the deck and complete the cut a few times. He then cuts off about half the deck and riffle shuffles the two halves together. Spread the pack out face up to show how well mixed the cards are. As you do, find any two adjacent cards of the same color near the center of the deck. Cut the deck between these cards and complete the cut.

Square up the pack and turn it face down. Thumb off four cards and hand them to the first spectator. Thumb off four more and hand them to the second spectator. Continue to give four-card packets to each of the participating spectators. We will assume there are five spectators. For ease of explanation we'll refer to the spectators as A, B, C, D, E, from left to right.

Ask each spectator to mix his four cards and select any one from his face-down packet. He is to place it face down on the table. No one knows which card he chose.

When this has been done, tell the spectators to mix their cards. Then each looks at the faces of his three cards. Point out that the packets can consist of three cards of the same color or of two cards of one color and a card of opposite color. Say, "If they're all of the same color, select any one and place it face down on top of the one already on the table. But if you have one card of one color and two of the opposite color, remove the *one* card that does *not* match the color of the other two." The spectator does this, placing his card face down on the table on top of the card already there.

After they have all done this, take the remaining two cards from each of them, making sure you collect them in order so that E's pair is on the bottom, D's on top of it, C's on top of that, B's on top of that and A's on top of all.

Beginning with the top card, upjog every other card. Strip out the upjogged cards as a group without disturbing their order and place this group on the table. As you do this, remark that you want to mix the cards.

Point out the odds against the tabled pairs being of the same color. Then turn up each pair to show that the odds have somehow been beaten, because each pair contains two cards of the same color. This is the first effect. You are about to follow it with an even stronger finish.

At this point you have five face-down cards in your hand. Say you will try and sense the colors of these cards without looking at the faces. Slowly you deal them into two heaps on the table, sometimes pausing as if having trouble with a particular card. What you really do is look at the face-up color pairs in front of the spectators and deal according to those colors, reading from A to E. For example, if the color pairs in front of the spectators read red, red, red, black, black, you would deal the first card into a heap on the left, then the next card into the same heap (because the color of B's matching cards is the same as A's). You would deal the third card into the same heap (because C's matching colors are the same as A's). You would deal the next card into a separate heap (because D's matching colors are different from A's) and you would deal the fifth card into the separate heap (because E's matching colors are different from A's). Thus you would deal the first three cards into one heap and the last two into a separate heap.

Pick up the other five-card packet on the table and simply repeat the process, beginning by dealing the first card into the left-hand heap, the next two into this heap, then the final two into the other heap.

You have dealt your ten cards into two separate heaps. Build up the impossibility of what you are attempting, then turn up each heap to show all blacks in one and all reds in the other.

40   REPLICA POKER

Ten cards are placed in a face-up row on the table as shown in Figure 18. The spectator is invited to slide out of the row any ace, any two, any three, any four and any five. When he has done this the other five cards are gathered in order from left to right. The spectator's cards are also gathered in order and placed alongside the other packet.

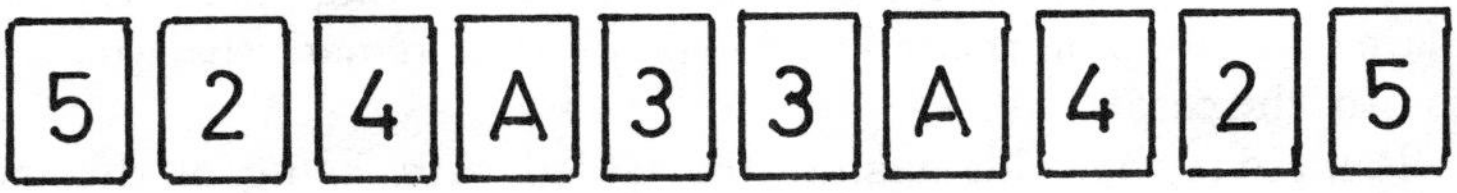

| 5 | 2 | 4 | A | 3 | 3 | A | 4 | 2 | 5 |

Fig. 18

Both poker hands contain identical cards, of course, but with a snap of the fingers the magician causes the cards in his hand to rearrange themselves in the same order as the spectator's cards.

METHOD: Remove the ace through five in spades and clubs. Deal them out exactly as shown in Figure 18. Then have the spectator remove any ace, two, three, four, five. His five cards can end up in any one of these 16 arrangements:

5 2 4 1 3	5 4 1 3 2
3 1 4 2 5	2 3 1 4 5
5 2 4 3 1	5 4 3 1 2
1 3 4 2 5	2 4 3 1 5
5 2 1 3 4	5 1 3 4 2
4 3 1 2 5	2 1 3 4 5
5 2 3 1 4	5 3 1 2 4
4 1 3 2 5	2 4 1 3 5

The spectator may, for example, draw out the five cards shown in Figure 19. After he does, gather his five cards from left to right, one card going on top of the next. Then gather the remaining five cards from left to right, one card going on top of the next. Turn your packet face down and place it alongside the spectator's packet.

Explain that in the game of Replica Poker the cards are compared one at a time. The player with the highest value card wins. You

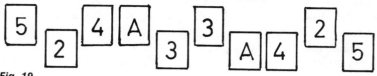

Fig. 19

further explain that you never lose even though you never win either.

Take the top card of your hand and the top card of the spectator's hand. Place them alongside one another. Turn the face-down card over and show that it has the same value as the face-up card. Repeat with each pair of cards. In each case the cards are the same.

Note that although the spectator can pick his poker hand in any one of 16 different ways, the remaining cards automatically arrange themselves in the same order. This is an example of something called a self-duplicating setup, used here in the context of a reverse or backward riffle shuffle. In other words, when the spectator slides five cards out of the row, he is unshuffling the packet. The setup itself then goes to work to insure that one packet will be in the same order as the other packet.

41 POSI-NEGATIVE CARDS

This is one of the strongest tricks that can be done with a riffle-shuffle setup. The basic effect was developed by several magicians. This handling was suggested by J. W. Sarles.

A spectator is asked to remove a deck of cards from its case, cut the pack a few times, and then give the deck a riffle shuffle. He then deals the deck into two heaps, one face up, one face down. He deals a card at a time off the top, dealing from left to right through the entire deck.

The spectator picks up the face-up packet and sorts it into two heaps according to color. The magician uses the face-down packet and follows the spectator's actions exactly, sorting his cards into two face-down heaps. For example, if the first three cards on the face of the spectator's packet were red, he would deal them into a heap on the left. The magician would deal three cards from the top of his face-down packet, sight unseen, into a heap near the spectator's. If the next five cards on the face of the spectator's packet were black, he would deal them into a separate heap on the right. The magician simultaneously deals the next five cards from the top of his face-down packet into a heap alongside the spectator's black heap.

The magician explains that the spectator has *visibly* separated his cards into reds and blacks. Because of the attraction the cards have for one another, the magician's cards have *invisibly* sorted themselves into reds and blacks. Turning over the face-down packets, the magician reveals that one contains nothing but red cards while the other contains nothing but black cards.

METHOD: Set up the deck so the colors alternate red-black-red-black from top to bottom. The spectator removes the deck from its case, cuts the deck and completes the cut. Then he cuts off about half the deck and riffle shuffles the two halves together.

Take back the deck and spread it face up to show the colors well mixed. Spot two cards of the same color that are adjacent to one another near the center. Cut the deck between these two cards and complete the cut. Then hand the deck back to the spectator.

He separates the deck into two packets, one face up and the other face down, by dealing the top card face down to the left, the next card face up to the right, the next face down to the left, and so on. Using the face-down packet, simply follow the spectator's actions as he sorts his face-up cards into reds and blacks. At the finish you will have two face-down heaps near his face-up heaps. Remark that your colors separated invisibly, then spread each of your heaps face up on the table to reveal all reds in one heap and all blacks in the other.

The fact that the spectator himself shuffled the deck makes this trick appear impossible. There is the further point that, when dealing the cards face up, the spectator sees that reds and blacks are randomly mixed. These two points combine to produce a stunning card effect using ordinary cards.

42   INCORPORATED COLOR CONTROL

The magician removes two cards from the deck, jots down a prediction on each, and then inserts the cards back into the pack. The pack is handed to a spectator for a riffle shuffle.

After he shuffles the cards, the spectator is told to deal pairs of cards face up off the top. Matching red pairs go into one heap, matching blacks into a separate heap, and red-black or non-matching pairs go into a third heap.

When he comes to the pair containing one of the prediction cards, the spectator reads it aloud. It says: "You have just dealt the fourth and last matching pair of blacks. However———"

The prediction is correct. The spectator has *just* dealt the fourth matching pair of black cards. It is not known if this is the last such pair because that can't be verified until the end of the trick, but the rest of the prediction can't be read until the spectator comes to the second half of the prediction.

He continues dealing pairs of cards off the top of the deck, sorting them into the proper heaps as before. Ultimately he comes to the second half of the prediction. It reads: "———you are destined to deal two more matching pairs and both will be red."

The spectator deals pairs of cards until he has dealt through the entire deck. The second prediction is indeed correct. He did deal two more matching pairs and both were red.

METHOD: Stack the deck as follows. The top half is arranged red-black-red-black and so on from top to bottom. The bottom half is arranged five blacks—red—3 blacks—five reds—black—♠2—black—red—black—red—♣2—five reds from top to bottom.

To present the trick, remove the ♠2 from the deck, jot down the first prediction ("You have just dealt the fourth and last matching pair of black cards. However———"), and return the ♠2 to its original position in the pack. Then remove the ♣2; jot down the second prediction ("———you are destined to deal two more matching pairs and both will be red"), and return the ♣2 to its original position in the pack. Split the deck at its midpoint. Let the spectator riffle shuffle the two halves together once. He then deals as already explained.

The outcome is automatic.

43   WHY YOU CAN'T WIN

People are fascinated with demonstrations of cheating. This routine exploits the fact that many people believe that if they shuffle and deal the cards it would be impossible for anyone to cheat. In this demonstration you show conclusively that the game is always under your control even though you don't handle the cards.

For best results you should have three spectators participate, though the trick can be carried out if there are fewer participants. One spectator shuffles and deals, another plays the part of the banker and one spectator will be your partner. As the game progresses it becomes clear that the dealer is going to lose on every round even though he shuffled and dealt the cards.

Before presenting the game, arrange the deck so the colors alternate red-black-red-black from top to bottom. This is the only preparation.

When the spectators are seated around the table, remark that it's possible to cheat even though you never shuffle or deal the cards. As you patter, remove the deck from its case. Cut it at about its midpoint, making sure there is a red card on the face of one half of the deck and a black card on the face of the other. Place the two packets face down on the table in front of the volunteer dealer.

Have him riffle shuffle the two halves of the deck together and square up the pack. Then tell him to deal out four packets of cards. He deals four hands in the conventional way, dealing from right to left in order. He continues the deal until he has gone through the entire deck. There will be four packets on the table, each containing 13 cards. From left to right the packets will be referred to as *A, B, C, D.*

Tell the dealer to take *A* for himself. Turn *B* face up and give it to the banker, explaining that these face-up cards will serve as poker chips or betting markers. Whoever wins a round gets one face-up card. At the end of the game the winner is the one with the most face-up cards.

Take packet *C* for yourself and give packet *D* to your partner. Before proceeding, make it clear that you and your partner are going to win and that the dealer is positively going to lose on every round, even though he shuffled and dealt the cards.

The game is this. On each round each player takes the top card of his packet and places it face up on the table. Two of the three cards must be the same color. The player who holds the odd-color card is the winner. Thus if the dealer turns up a black card and you turn up a red card and your partner turns up a black card, you would win because you have the odd-color card on that round.

On each round the banker gives the winner a card from the face-up packet. If all three players deal a card of the same color, the round is a draw and no one wins. The game appears fair, yet the dealer will not win a single round.

Using giant cards available in magic shops, you can perform this routine from the platform or stage. Give the banker a top hat and give the dealer a green visor. This makes it easier for the audience to follow the action. The game is a graphic example of why you can't win at the other man's game, even if you shuffle and deal the cards.

TWO-DECK CARD TRICKS

The premise of the two-deck trick is that if each of two parties gets a deck of cards and each chooses a card in the same way, then each person will choose the same card.

This simple premise is responsible for the development of some of the most intriguing card routines. In such tricks the presentation is important. Stress that it is possible for two minds to operate on the same wavelength. When the trick is brought to a successful conclusion the spectator can only conclude that it was the result of an amazing coincidence or a demonstration of genuine mind reading.

44 HYPNOTISN'T

In this routine one spectator gets a red-backed deck and the other spectator gets a blue-backed deck. Each chooses two cards in a random way using his own deck. Although neither spectator appears to have been influenced by the other, when the two chosen cards are turned over, it is found that the spectators chose exactly the same two cards.

METHOD: Prior to the performance of the trick, arrange to have the ♠5 on top of each deck and the ♥9 on the bottom of each deck.

To present the routine, patter about the fact that on occasion two minds can operate on the same channel or the same frequency. To illustrate, remove each deck from its case. Each spectator takes a deck and holds it face down in his left hand. Now ask each spectator to lift off about a quarter of his deck, turn it over and place it face up on top of the balance of the deck. Then each spectator lifts up about half of his deck, turns it over and places it on top of the balance of the deck. Finally, each spectator cuts his deck at about the midpoint and completes the cut.

In performing the above actions the spectators should strive to follow one another as closely as possible. This is in keeping with the idea that if they perform the same actions at the same time, they will choose the same cards.

Have each spectator spread his deck on the table. There will be a face-up group of cards in the center of the deck. Tell each spectator to remove the face-down card directly to the left of the face-up group, and the face-down card directly to the right of the face-up group. The result is shown in Figure 20.

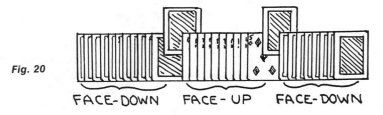

Fig. 20

FACE-DOWN   FACE-UP   FACE-DOWN

Each spectator turns over his two cards. It is seen that both spectators have chosen the same cards.

45   THE JAKS TWO-DECK TRICK

This trick by Stanley Jaks is a classic of contemporary card magic. The routine will be described as Jaks originally presented it, with a third deck used to obtain an additional effect, but you will see that even without the third deck the routine is exceptional.

The performer gives two decks of cards to two spectators. One deck has red backs and the other has blue backs. While these decks are being removed from their cases and shuffled by the spectators, the magician gives a third deck to another member of the audience to hold.

One of the assisting spectators takes one deck for himself and pockets it. The performer takes the other deck and pockets it. Each person reaches into his pocket and removes one card. The selected cards are exchanged and placed into opposite decks. Thus the chosen red-backed card ends up in the blue-backed deck, and the chosen blue-backed card ends up in the red-backed deck.

Both people now remove the decks from their pockets. The odd-backed card in each deck is turned face up. They prove to be the same card!

The magician then turns to the spectator who holds the third deck. He spells the name of the chosen card, dealing a card off the top for each letter. When he gets to the last letter he turns over that card. It matches the two chosen cards!

METHOD: Prior preparation is simple and the trick is foolproof, yet the simple means produces a tremendously effective mental mystery with cards.

Before presenting the trick, remove the ♦5 from each deck and place these two cards in the right jacket pocket. The blue-backed ♦5 should be closest to the body. Return each deck to its case.

In a third deck place the ♦5 in a position fourteenth from the top of the deck. Case this deck and you are ready.

To present the routine, hand the red-backed deck to one spectator, the blue-backed deck to another. Ask each person to shuffle his deck. Hand the cased third deck to another spectator. Tell him to hold onto it for safekeeping until the end of the trick.

Ask one of the spectators to take the red-backed deck and place it in his outside right jacket pocket. You take the blue-backed deck and place it in your right jacket pocket so that the two ♦5's in the pocket will be on the bottom or face of the deck.

Have the spectator remove any card from the red-backed deck. He does not look at this card. You pretend to remove a random card from your deck, but really remove the blue-backed ♦5 and place it face down on the table.

Take the spectator's card from him. Give him your card. Tell him to place your card in the center of his deck. Pretend to place his card in the center of your deck. Actually place it on the bottom of the blue-backed deck. Then place the red-backed ♦5 in the center of the blue-backed deck.

Remove your pack but leave the red-backed indifferent card in the pocket. Have the spectator remove his deck. Each of you spread your pack and outjog the odd-color card. Have them turned over to reveal that you both chose the ♦5.

For the added climax call attention to the spectator holding the third deck. Have him remove the deck from its case and hold it face down in his left hand. Then ask him to spell F-I-V-E-O-F-D-I-A-M-O-N-D-S, dealing a card for each letter. He turns up the last card and it is the ♦5.

J. W. Sarles added several touches to this routine. At the start he would arrange to have keys or coins in the pocket that also contained the two ♦ 5's. As the trick began, he asked the spectator to empty his right jacket pocket. Of course Sarles did the same, removing everything except the two cards. The subtle point here is that in emptying his pocket of keys he implied that the pocket must be otherwise empty.

In the Sarles handling the spectator was given a choice of either deck. This may seem a small point but it adds to the impression of fairness of the handling. After cards were chosen and exchanged, the deck was brought out of the pocket but the indifferent card was on the bottom of the pack. In other words, the indifferent card was not left in the pocket.

After the two odd-backed cards were outjogged, Sarles would take both decks, holding them so that the outjogged odd-backed cards faced the spectator. The spectator removed a card with each hand and then turned both cards face up to reveal that both were the ♦ 5. Finally, Sarles would place his deck on top of the spectator's deck and put both aside. By doing this, the indifferent card at the bottom of the performer's deck was quietly added to the top of the spectator's desk. All could now be left with the audience.

In the Jaks method the preparation does not involve the decks, so either deck may be used for other tricks. At any time in the performance you are ready to do the Jaks two-deck trick.

46 THE DREAM DECK

If you do not have two decks handy to perform the Jaks two-deck trick, there is a subtle variation that uses only one deck. In this trick the spectator picks a card from a packet he holds behind his back. You pick a card from a packet you hold behind your back. When the chosen cards are compared, it turns out they are the black fives. The kicker is that they are the *only* black cards in both packets. All the other cards are red.

METHOD: Take any borrowed, shuffled deck and hold it so you alone can see the faces. Beginning at the face of the deck, upjog the first 13 red cards you come to. Strip them out of the deck without showing their faces and place the packet face down before the spectator.

Upjog any black card near the face of the balance of the deck.

Then upjog all of the remaining red cards as well as the mate of the black card. If the black card is the ♠5, upjog the other black five —the ♣5. Strip this packet out of the deck and place the balance of the deck aside.

Place the two mating black fives on the bottom of your packet. Then place your packet behind your back. Instruct the spectator to place his packet behind his back. When the cards are out of sight, each of you mixes your cards. Actually you do nothing. The spectator is asked to remove any card from his packet. You remove the bottom card.

Exchange cards with the spectator. Tell him to place your card behind his back, turn it face up, and then insert it reversed in his packet. Pretend to do the same with his card, but simply place it on top of your packet. Take the black five from the bottom of the packet, turn it face up, and insert it into the center of the packet.

Each person brings his packet into view. The packets are spread face down to show that each of you chose a black five. Then have the remaining cards turned face up to reveal the even more remarkable fact that both of you chose the only black cards in the packet.

47   THE CLUELESS CARD TRICK

This version of the two-deck trick is a bit different. Here each of two spectators chooses cards from a single deck. The magician then chooses two cards which prove to be the same cards chosen by the spectators. The routine is based on a card problem devised by the British magician E. G. Brown. There is no preparation and no force. The spectators may choose any two cards.

Have a spectator shuffle the deck until he is satisfied that you could not possibly know any card. Then have him divide the deck into three approximately equal piles. We'll call the piles *A*, *B* and *C*.

Have the spectator take pile *A*, shuffle it and take some of the cards for himself. He gives the rest of pile *A* to the second spectator. It does not matter how many cards each person has. Turn your back and have each person silently count the number of cards in his possession. Point out that you could not possibly know how many cards either person holds.

There are still two piles on the table. Pick up pile *B*. Turn to the first spectator and explain that you are going to deal cards one at a time onto the table. He is to note a card at a position corresponding to the number of cards he holds. Thus, for example, if he holds eight cards, he would note the eighth card you deal.

Hold the pile of cards face down in the left hand. Take the top card, call it "One," and show it to the spectator. Then deal it face down onto the table. Take the next card, call it "Two," show it to the spectator and deal it onto the card you just dealt to the table. Continue in this way until all of the cards have been dealt. Remember how many cards are in the pile. Assume there are 17 cards in pile *B*. At the completion of the deal have the spectator place his small packet of cards on top of this pile.

Now pick up pile *C*. Turn to the second spectator. Explain that you are going to deal the cards one at a time. He is to note and remember the card at a position corresponding to the number of cards he holds. If he holds 11 cards, he would silently remember the eleventh card you deal.

Deal the way you did with pile *B*. Remember how many cards are in pile *C*. Say there are 20. Have the second spectator drop his packet on top of pile *C*.

Turn now to the first spectator. Remark that you too have decided on two numbers and that you will choose cards the same way the spectators did. Pick up the group of cards at *B*. Recall that there were originally 17 cards at *B*. Count down to the seventeenth card, remove this card and place it face down on the table near the first spectator.

Pick up the group of cards at *C*. Recall that pile *C* originally contained 20 cards. Count silently to the twentieth card and place it near the second spectator.

Have the spectators name their cards. Then remark that since you chose cards in the same way, it should follow that you chose the same cards. Turn over each of your cards to reveal a perfect match.

48 CRISS CROSS

The ingenious exploitation of an offbeat principle makes this one of the best tricks with two decks of cards. It is suggested for use after a trick like the Jaks Two-Deck Trick (No. 45). This trick is a simplified version of a famous George Sands routine. The effect is something of a novelty in that nothing magical happens to the cards. Rather, something happens to the spectator that makes it impossible for him to carry out a simple procedure.

The nines through aces are removed from a deck. Using just these 24 cards, you show the spectator a simple way to sort the colors. He finds it easy to do, but then you say that it will never work for him again, and with a snap of the fingers you make it impossible for him to succeed.

METHOD: Two decks are used. Both may be borrowed, as there is no preparation. One deck is red-backed and the other deck blue-backed. Hand the red-backed deck to the spectator and instruct him to remove the nines, tens, jacks, queens, kings and aces. While he does this, pick up the blue-backed deck. Fan the cards with the faces to you. Find two adjacent cards that have values of nine or higher. You may find a jack adjacent to an ace, or a nine adjacent to a queen. Cut these two cards to the top of the deck. If you don't find two such cards, simply place two of them on top of the pack.

Beginning at the face of the blue-backed deck, run through the cards and upjog all cards having a value of nine or higher. Do not upjog the top two cards.

Remove these upjogged 22 cards and place them on the table. This packet will be used at the beginning of the demonstration. Place the balance of the blue-backed deck aside.

When the spectator has removed all of the cards having a value of nine or higher from his deck (a total of 24 cards) tell him to place these cards on top of the red-backed deck for the moment.

Explain that you will show him a simple way to sort colors. As you patter, pick up the blue-backed packet and sort the cards according to color, blacks in one heap, reds in the other, as in Figure 21.

Fig. 21

REDS   BLACKS

Remove the face card of each heap and place it above the heap, as in Figure 22. Then remove the next card of each heap, cross the hands and place the cards on opposite color heaps, as in Figure 23.

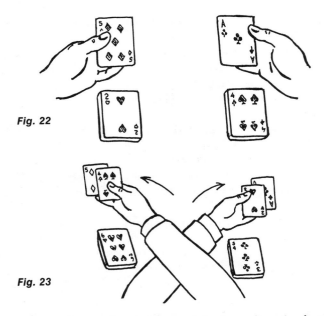

Fig. 22

Fig. 23

The next cards are placed on top of the heap directly above them (referring to Figure 23, the ♥6 would go on the ♠4 and the ♣3 on top of the ♥2). Then the next cards are picked up, the hands crossed and the cards dropped on opposite heaps.

This alternating procedure continues until all cards from the original two heaps have been transferred. The result is two new heaps in which the colors alternate. Turn each packet face down. Then place one packet on top of the other. Finally, deal the combined heap into two packets. Deal alternately as if dealing two hands for a card game. After all cards have been dealt, turn both packets face up and spread the cards. One heap contains all reds and the other heap contains all blacks. This result is not surprising. Indeed, the spectator will have anticipated it.

The spectator is asked if he can duplicate the feat. He tries, following the above procedure, and is successful. He repeats it to be certain he knows the procedure. Then he tries it one more time just to be sure. Each time he mixes the cards as in Figures 22 and 23, deals the mixed cards into two heaps, and successfully separates the colors. Since the procedure is so simple and obvious, he may even wonder why you are doing it at all, and this is exactly what you want him to think.

After the final try, have the spectator pick up the two heaps, shuffle them together, and drop them back onto the top of the blue-backed deck. When he's done this say, "Now I want you to try it with the red-backed cards."

Have him remove the top 24 cards from the red-backed deck. He is to separate them into two heaps, blacks in one heap, reds in the other. After he's done this, say, "The combination of red-backed and blue-backed cards has a curious effect on the mind. Before we started I gave you a subconscious instruction which allowed you to separate the colors. But when we switched to a different deck, the subconscious instruction was destroyed. You will never again separate the colors."

The spectator goes through the procedure of Figures 22 and 23 to mix the colors, he places one packet on top of the other, then he deals them into two heaps. The colors should separate but, oddly enough, they don't. He can try again, but the colors still refuse to separate.

Sooner or later it will occur to him that even if the trick won't work with the red-backed cards, it *must* work with the blue-backed cards. He removes the nines through aces from the top of the blue-backed deck, unaware that he is using the original 22 cards *plus* the two cards you left on top of the deck at the start. He tries to sort the colors using blue-backed cards. The trick should work but, to his amazement, it won't.

49 JUMPBACK

This final routine introduces a paradox to the format of the traditional two-deck trick. If you perform a two-deck trick on some occasion, and on a later occasion are asked to repeat the trick, this is a good routine to do because it seems as if you are doing a standard two-deck trick right up to the last second. Then things take a strange turn. It is the author's solution to a challenging problem.

A spectator choose a card from a red-backed deck and signs his name on the face of the card. Say the card is the ♠4. This card is returned to the red-backed deck. The spectators see it going into the center of the pack, and the red-backed pack is not touched again.

Then another spectator chooses a card from the blue-backed deck. Although he had no idea which card was chosen by the first spectator, he is surprised to find that he too has chosen the ♠4.

The odd point is that although the ♠4 is undeniably blue-backed, although it came from the blue-backed deck, it bears the first spectator's signature! Thus, not only did the second spectator choose the same card, his card turns out to have the same signature.

METHOD: Place the red-backed ♠4 second from the face or bottom of the blue-backed deck. Place the blue-backed ♠4 second from the bottom of the red-backed deck, as in Figure 24. Put each deck in its own case. This completes the preparation.

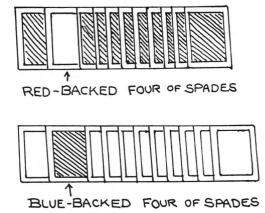

RED-BACKED FOUR OF SPADES

Fig. 24

BLUE-BACKED FOUR OF SPADES

When ready to perform, open the blue-backed card case and remove the blue-backed deck. Be careful not to spread the cards accidentally because this might reveal the red-backed card. The easiest way to conceal the presence of the red-backed ♠4 is to remove the deck face up.

Place the blue-backed deck face up on the table to your left, with the card case above it, as in Figure 25. The card just in back of the ♦2 in Figure 25 is the odd-backed ♠4.

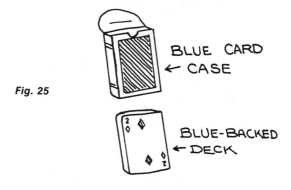

BLUE CARD
← CASE

Fig. 25

BLUE-BACKED
← DECK

Ask one of the volunteer spectators to leave the room, explaining that you will call him back later. When he is gone, remove the red-backed deck from its case. Make sure the deck is face up when you remove it. This insures that no one will spot the blue-backed ♠4 in the deck.

Tell the spectator at the table to give you a number between one and 15. Explain that you will count the number twice, once for him and once for the spectator in the other room.

Say he gives you eight. With the red-backed deck face up in the left hand, deal the face card onto the table, then deal the next card to the right of it. Deal the next card onto the left-hand heap and deal the next card onto the right-hand heap. Continue dealing in this way, a card to each heap alternately, until you have dealt eight cards.

Pick up the leftmost heap and place it on top of the rightmost heap. Place the combined heap back onto the face of the deck. Say, "As I mentioned, we deal once for him and once for you. That deal was for him. This one is for you." Deal eight cards off the face of the deck into a face-up heap. The eighth card you deal will be the ♠4.

Place the ♠4 face up on the table in front of the spectator. Ask him to sign his name in the center of the card. As he does, gather the cards you dealt and replace them on the face of the red-backed deck. Then place the red-backed deck face down on the table.

Take the signed ♠4 from the spectator and drop it face up onto the face of the blue-backed deck. Openly cut the blue-backed deck and complete the cut as you say, "If we were to spread this pack face up for the selection of another card, the person would see your signature on the face."

Turn the blue-backed deck face down and spread it between the hands. A red-backed card will show up in the center of the deck. Say, "If we spread it face down for the selection of a card, he will know your card because it has a different-color back." Cut the deck and complete the cut so the red-backed card is on top.

Remove the red-backed card, taking care not to flash the face. Then insert it face down into the face-down red-backed deck so that about a quarter of it protrudes from one end, as in Figure 26. Say, "The only way to hide your card from him is to return it to its own deck." Lift the red-backed deck with the left hand, as in Figure 27, to show the face of the ♠4. The audience sees just the upper index corner of the ♠4 and is thus unaware that it is not the signed card.

Tap the card square with the deck and place the red-backed deck to one side. The audience is convinced that the signed card has been returned to its own deck.

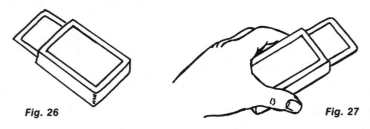

Fig. 26   **Fig. 27**

Ask that the spectator in the next room now return. When he has joined the other guests, ask him for a number between one and 15. At times he will unknowingly choose the same number as the first spectator. If he does, play up the point, remarking that he must be on the same wavelength.

Assume that he chose the number 11. Hold the blue-backed deck face down in the left hand. Deal 11 cards onto the table. Deal the same way you did the first time, alternating a card to each of two packets, dealing from left to right, until you have dealt a total of 11 cards. Then place the leftmost packet on top of the rightmost packet and place the combined packet on top of the deck.

Say, "We deal twice, once for him and once for you. The first deal was for him. This one is for you." Deal 11 cards off the top of the deck. Place the eleventh card aside. Notice that the dealing procedure is the same as for the red-backed deck except that here the deal is done with the cards face down.

Insert the chosen card sideways into the deck and hold it as shown in Figure 28. Slowly turn the deck face up as you say, "You happened to choose the very same card as this fellow."

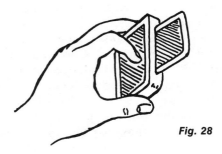

Fig. 28

This appears to be the conclusion of the effect. The audience can see the face of the chosen card. It is the ♠4. But because the card is in the deck, they can't see the initials. Thus they assume the point of the trick is that the second spectator chose the same card as the first spectator, in itself an impressive feat.

Say, "Not only is it the same card . . ." Pause here for dramatic effect. Then add, ". . . it has the same signature."

Remove the ♠4 from the deck to show that it has somehow acquired the first spectator's signature. This is an unexpected ending to a strong coincidence trick.

TOPOLOGICAL CARD TRICKS

The tricks in this chapter use cards that are torn or folded. This may seem a slender premise on which to base a chapter, but topological card tricks represent an offbeat approach that generates surprising and different card effects.

Most topological card tricks require gimmicks or manipulation that lie outside the scope of this book. The tricks in this brief chapter have been chosen because they are easy to perform and provide something of the flavor of this unique area of card magic.

50 THE HOUSE THAT JACK BUILT

The magician makes an impromptu card house out of three playing cards by folding them in half, as in Figure 29, and assembling them on top of the card case. Figures 30 and 31 show how the card house is constructed.

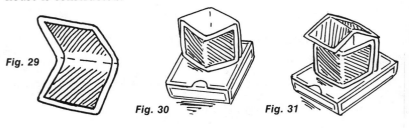

Fig. 29

Fig. 30

Fig. 31

A spectator tries to guess the address of the card house. Whatever number he calls out, this number is used to aid in the selection of a card. His card may be a jack. The jack vanishes from the deck and is found in the card case *under* the card house. For the finish, the house is shown to indeed be the house that Jack built because all of the cards that went into its construction turn out to be jacks.

METHOD: Beforehand arrange to have three jacks on top of the deck and the fourth jack thirteenth from the top. Say this jack is the ♣J. In the card case is a duplicate ♣J from a matching deck.

Remove the top three cards from the deck and fold them in half as in Figure 29. Try not to show the faces of these three cards to the audience. Place two of them together on top of the card case as shown in Figure 30 to form the walls of the card house. Then use the third folded card to form the roof. The finished card house is shown in Figure 31. Point to the card case under the card house and remark that the card case represents the finished basement.

Ask a spectator to guess the address or street number of the card house, adding that the street number is between ten and 20. Whatever number he names, deal that many cards off the top of the deck. Assume the number is 14. After you have dealt 14 cards, say to the spectator, "The number 14 is made up of two digits, a 1 and a 4." Deal one card onto the table to represent the 1 in his number. Then deal four cards onto the table for the 4 in his number. Hand him the last card dealt and ask him to remember this card. It will be the ♣J.

Tell him to put his card onto the top of the deck. Then have him pick up all of the dealt cards and place them on top of his card. Take the deck behind your back and say you will try to find his card. Unknown to the audience, at this point his card will be tenth from the top. Silently deal nine cards from top to bottom, then slip the tenth under your belt in the back. Remove the next card, take it into view but don't show it. Look at this card and say, "Did you pick the jack of clubs?" When the spectator says yes, bring the deck out and insert the supposed ♣J into the center. Say, "That's funny because the address you gave me, the number 14, is the address of the house that jacks built." As you say this, remove the three cards that make up the card house and show that they are all jacks.

"Even more amazing, the other brother, the jack of clubs, lives in the basement." Open the card case and remove the ♣J. The audience can look through the deck but there is nothing to find.

51 MOVING PARTS

The effect briefly is that four cards are torn in half and mixed, yet the halves of each card correctly and instantly find their mating halves.

Preparation is simple. Tear or cut a slit in the ♠A, ♠2, and ♠3, tearing from one side across to the center as shown in Figure 32.

Fig. 32

Slide the cards together as shown in Figure 33 so that the ♠2 and ♠3 slide into the slit in the ♠A. Another view is shown in Figure 34. Square up the packet, turn it end for end and hold it in the left hand, then place the ♠4 face down on top.

Fig. 33   **Fig. 34**

Hold the packet fairly deep in the left hand so that if you raise the packet for the spectator to see the faces, he can see the ♠A but not the slit in the middle of the packet. A spectator's view is shown in Figure 35.

With the right forefinger, slowly riffle the upper right corners of the cards one at a time, as in Figure 36, so that the spectator gets a clear view of the four cards. This shows him that the cards are in numerical order.

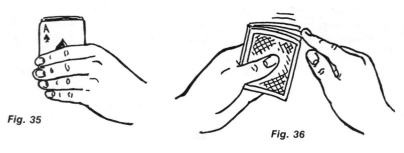

Fig. 35

Fig. 36

Then fold the four-card packet in half, as in Figure 37, straighten it out and tear it across the middle. This gives you a packet of eight half-cards. Hold them together with the left hand as shown in Figure 38. It is important that the packet should not get turned end-for-end during the tearing process. If you look at the faces of the half-card packets, as in the exposed view of Figure 39, the ♠A should be at the top and the ♠2 at the bottom.

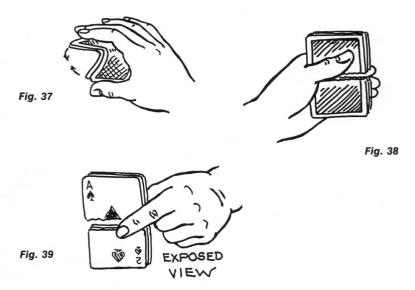

Fig. 37

Fig. 38

Fig. 39   EXPOSED VIEW

Holding the packets face down as in Figure 38, use the right thumb and first finger to deal the top card of the top (or outer) half-card packet onto the table. Then deal the top card of the bottom (or inner) half-card packet just below it onto the table. These are the two halves of the ♠4.

Deal the top card of the top half-card packet to the right of the first half-card. Then deal the top card of the bottom half-card packet under that. Continue in this way with the remaining half-cards.

Turn up the half-cards in the upper row. The result will look like Figure 40. Note that these half-cards are in correct numerical order, so all appears fair. Exchange A with B, then exchange the half-card at B with the half-card at C. These exchanges are made with the face-down half-cards only. It appears as if all the half-cards are mixed. Snap the fingers, then turn up each of the face-down pieces in place. Matching halves are back in their correct position. You will find this an odd and puzzling trick, unlike almost all other card tricks both in terms of effect and in terms of method.

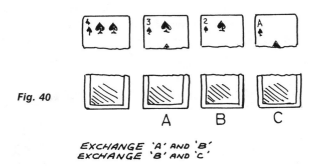

Fig. 40

EXCHANGE 'A' AND 'B'
EXCHANGE 'B' AND 'C'

In presenting this trick it is easy to gimmick the ♠A, ♠2 and ♠3 during the course of some other card trick. Do any trick that requires that you place the deck behind the back. With the deck out of sight it is an easy matter silently to tear a slit across the ♠A, ♠2 and ♠3. Return these three cards to the deck until ready to perform. Then place the deck below the level of the tabletop, remove the ace through four of spades, and arrange them as in Figure 33.

When doing tricks like this one, make sure you use your own cards, and an old deck at that. With rare exceptions people don't like having their own cards torn up, so be sure you use an expendable deck.

52   THE LINKING CARDS

In *Amusements in Mathematics* (Dover 20473-1) H. E. Dudeney describes "The Cardboard Chain," a puzzle in which each cardboard link is solid. In some older books the piece of cardboard is a playing card. The following is the author's version, in which two playing cards magically link together. The cards are solid and there are no gimmicks.

As seen by the audience, you tear the center from each of two cards, Figure 41. The cards are then opened out, as in Figure 42, and placed under a handkerchief. The magician makes a mystic adjustment and then brings the cards into view to show them linked, as in Figure 43.

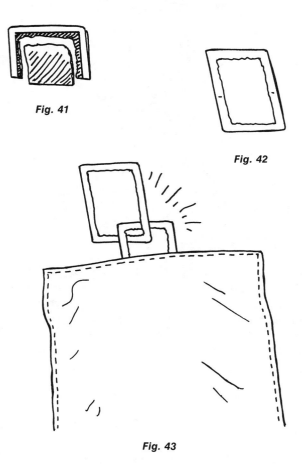

Fig. 41

Fig. 42

Fig. 43

The cards are then unlinked under the handkerchief and handed out for examination. The cards may be borrowed and marked by the spectators. You use only two cards and there is no prior preparation.

METHOD: After the centers of the cards have been cut out and discarded, place the two cards under a large handkerchief or scarf. Secretly fold one of the cards in half across its original fold line or crease. Slide the other card over it so the two cards are "linked," and hold them in place as shown in Figure 44. The card held by the left fingertips is actually the card folded in half across the middle. The fingertips hold the card flat on the table and keep it from unfolding.

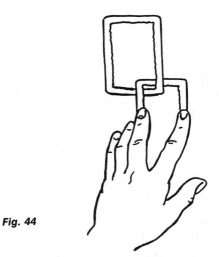

Fig. 44

While the left hand holds the linked cards in position, the right hand draws the handkerchief back far enough to expose the linked condition, as in Figure 43. The cards are then covered again.

Unlink them under the handkerchief, straighten out the folded card, and bring both cards out for examination.

The trick may also be done with borrowed business cards or with play money.

CARD-FORCING SECRETS

Most of the chapters in this book group card routines according to effect. This chapter represents an important exception because here effects are grouped according to method, specifically, techniques used to force a card on the spectator.

In the best forces the spectator seems to have an unlimited choice in selecting his card. Many force methods take place with the deck in the spectator's hands. He thinks he has control over the cards, yet you compel him to choose the card you want him to pick.

Here is a collection of some of the best force methods. Each is tied in with an application so the reader can see how the force is worked into an effect. Other force methods are described throughout this book. These methods are fundamental to an understanding of card magic. Study them and you will have on hand important and powerful techniques.

53 THE X-FORCE

From a borrowed, shuffled deck the magician removes the two red jacks. The spectator then cuts the deck anywhere and removes the card cut to. This card is placed between the jacks. When it is removed, it is seen to have changed into a jack.

The basic method is known as the X-Force because the packets are placed on top of one another at right angles to form an X. Basically you are going to force the top card of the deck by a seemingly fair process. It would be too obvious to force the card and then reveal it, so the conclusion of the trick is delayed, making it seem as if a freely chosen card placed between two jacks is caused to change to a jack.

When you get the deck, turn it face up and begin to look through it for two cards. Glimpse the top card of the deck. Whatever it is, remove two cards of the same value but of opposite color. In our example the top card of the deck is a black jack. Remove the two red jacks from the deck and place them face down on the table.

To force the top card, place the deck face down on the table in front of the spectator. Have him cut off about half. In Figure 45 he has cut off packet A. You then place packet B on top of it, but at right angles, as in Figure 46.

Fig. 45

Fig. 46

It is not wise to have the spectator take a card immediately. Instead, call attention to the two cards you removed from the deck. Turn them face up to show they are the red jacks.

Now have the spectator take the top card of packet A in Figure 46. You can lift packet B away to make it easier for him to take the top card of A. It appears as if he is taking the card he cut to, but really the top card of packet A is the original top card of the deck.

Place his card, sight unseen, between the face-up red jacks. Square up the three-card packet, snap the fingers, then deal out the three cards. Turn up his card to show that it has changed to a jack.

54 HORNSWOGGLED

A packet of cards is removed from the deck. The spectator takes a small group of cards from the top of the packet, shuffles them and secretly counts them. Only he knows the number of cards in the packet.

The magician openly transfers ten cards from the top of the packet to the bottom. Then he has the spectator replace his group of cards on top. Then the magician openly transfers another ten cards from top to bottom.

The spectator looks at the top card of the packet. Then he places it at the same position from the top as the number of cards in the group he cut off originally. If he cut off five cards originally, he would place the chosen card fifth from the top.

The magician does not know how many cards the spectator took originally, so he hasn't a clue as to the present location of the chosen card. Yet without asking a question, the magician deals cards off the top of the packet into a face-up heap and correctly stops on the very card chosen by the spectator.

METHOD: This trick is an example of a means of forcing a card that lies in a particular position in the deck. In this case you are going to force the bottom card of a packet by an underhanded means.

Beforehand secretly note the top card of the deck. Count 21 cards off the top into a heap, thus reversing their order. Proceed with the trick exactly as described. The spectator must arrive at the secretly noted card.

To say it another way, whatever card is on the bottom of the 21-card packet, the spectator will choose this card. All of the mumbo jumbo prior to this merely keeps the trick from looking too simple.

55 COLOROTO

A subtle force devised by Lin Searles is combined here with a previously unpublished method for quickly determining the suit of a chosen card. Preparation consists of placing a club, a heart and a spade, in that order, in your jacket pocket. Then place the four fours on top of the deck.

To present the trick, hold the deck face down in the left hand. Invite a spectator to cut off a packet of any size and turn it face up, as in Figure 47. He then places the face-up packet on top of the face-down cards in your left hand.

Fig. 47

The left hand is palm up at this point. Turn the left hand palm down and spread the cards from left to right on the table, as in Figure 48. There will be a group of face-up cards on the right followed by a group of face-down cards on the left.

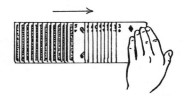

Fig. 48

Say, "We will use the first four face-down cards." Slide the face-up cards away. Let the spectator remove the first four face-down cards on the face-down portion of the deck. That is, going from the right end of the deck toward the left end, he removes the first four face-down cards he comes to. Unknown to him, these are the four fours.

Keeping the four cards face down, he mixes them thoroughly, places one in his pocket and returns the others to the deck. The deck is assembled face down. The spectator then shuffles it and hands it to you.

Drop the deck into the pocket containing the three cards you placed there earlier. While you turn your back, have the spectator look at and remember the card in his pocket. He then returns the card to his pocket so it remains hidden from view.

You know he chose a four, but you don't know which one. By asking just two questions, you will correctly pinpoint the suit of the chosen four. This is the author's method of determining the correct suit and is handled as follows.

Remark that you will use random cards to focus the spectator's mind. Reach into the pocket and remove the club card. Hold it so the spectator can see the face. Turn your head aside so it is clear you cannot see the card. Ask, "Is your chosen card the same color as this card?"

After he answers, return this card to your pocket. Then remove the heart and the spade together. Show them to the spectator, keeping your head turned aside, and ask, "Was your card the same suit as either of these cards?"

After the spectator answers, return these two cards to your pocket. You are now ready to name the chosen card.

The first card you held up was a club and you asked if the spectator's card was the same color as that card. If he said yes, you know he picked a black card. If he said no, he picked a red card. Thus you know the color of his card.

When you bring the heart and the spade out, it looks as if you reached into the deck and brought out two random cards. With your head turned aside ask the spectator if his card is the same suit as either of these cards.

Since you know the color of his card, his answer to this question will tell you the suit. Thus if you know the card is black and he says one of these cards is the same suit as his card, you know he picked a spade. If the card is black and he doesn't see a card of the same suit, you know his card was a club.

If his card is red and he says one of the cards in your hand is the same suit as his card, you know he chose a heart. If his card is red but he says he doesn't see a card of the same suit in your hand, he chose a diamond.

Since the value of his card is four, you then go on to name the value and suit of the chosen card. The deck may then be examined as there is nothing to find.

The key to success here lies in the fact that you apparently do not know which cards you remove from the shuffled deck in your pocket. Note too that the trick can be done with just two cards in the pocket at the start, a club and a heart. Remove the club and ask if it is the same color as the chosen card. Then remove the club and the heart and ask if either of these cards is the same suit as the chosen card. The spectator's answers reveal the identity of his card.

56   CUT DEEPER

This excellent method was devised by Ed Balducci. Beforehand, spot the top card of the deck. This will be the force card. Hand the deck to the spectator and have him hold it face down in his left hand.

Instruct him to cut off about a quarter of the deck, turn it face up and place it on top of the balance of the deck. Then have him cut off about half the deck, turn it over and place it on top of the balance of the deck.

At this point there will be a group of face-up cards on top. Have the spectator remove the face-up cards. then tell him to look at the first face-down card. This will be the top card of the face-down portion in his left hand.

Although the cutting procedure seems fair and beyond your control, the card he arrived at will be the force card. No applications of this force will be given here, but for one routine incorporating the Balducci force, see "The Open Prediction" (No. 7).

57   ON THE LAM

This prediction effect is based on a force idea of Louis Lam. The magician successfully predicts the location of a chosen card. There is an additional surprise in that the chosen card has mysteriously turned itself face up in the deck.

To prepare the trick, place the ♠A on top of the deck. Then place a light pencil dot in the upper left corner of the card that lies thirteenth from the top of the deck. This preparation is done secretly prior to performance. The prepared deck is shown in Figure 49.

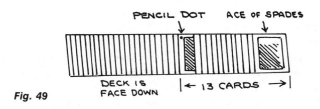

Fig. 49

Hold the deck face down in the left hand. Say, "I'm going to pick a card for myself and write something on it." Turn the top card (♠A) face up on top of the deck.

Pretend to concentrate for a moment, then write the number 13 on the face of the ♠A. Say, "I'll bury my card in the deck."

Leave the ♠A face up on top of the deck. With the left thumb push cards over to the right until you have pushed over the pencil-dotted card. The right hand takes this group of 13 cards as shown in Figure 50. Then the right hand turns palm down and places its packet back onto the deck.

Fig. 50

To check that the procedure has been correctly followed, at this point you should have 12 face-up cards on top of the deck, then the face-down ♠A, then the rest of the deck face down.

Spread the cards between the hands and have the spectator choose any face-down card. If he chooses the ♠A, pretend that this was the point of the trick and simply stop at this point because you are never going to top this. In the more likely case he will choose some card other than the ♠A.

When he has taken the card out of the deck, instruct him to look at the card and remember it. Place the balance of the deck on the table. The 12 face-up cards should still be at the top of the deck.

Tell him to place his chosen card face down on top of the deck. Then have him lift up about half the deck, Figure 51, turn it over and place it back onto the balance of the deck. His card is now buried in the pack at a location that neither of you know.

Fig. 51

Hand him the pack. Ask him to deal cards off the top until he comes to the ♠A. All of the cards he deals will be face-up cards. When he deals the ♠A off, remark that it is the last face-up card. Point out that you wrote the number 13 on it.

Have him deal 13 cards off the balance of the deck. These cards are all face down. When he gets to the thirteenth card it will be face up and it will be his card!

58   SPEAK OF THE DEVIL

After signing a pact with the Devil, the unwary victim is frequently offered a chance to double his money. The bet is simple. The Devil removes the 13 spades from the deck. He picks one of these cards for himself. A simple process of elimination is used to discard all of the remaining cards except one. If this card is higher than the Devil's card, the victim wins. Otherwise he loses. The ace is low; the king is high.

"Obviously, if I picked the king," the Devil says, "You couldn't pick a card that beats me. If I picked the seven, you would have an even chance of beating me.

"If I picked the six or the five, then you would have a better than even chance of choosing a card that beat me. But to make it an attractive offer, I'll choose a really low card, the three of spades."

The Devil (ably played by the magician) removes the ♠3 from the packet, leaving the other 12 spades.

"All you have to do is get a card that's higher than ♠3," the Devil says, "And we'll leave the process of elimination in your hands."

The process is this. The remaining 12 spaces are mixed face down. The spectator withdraws any two face-down cards. The magician chooses one of these two cards and discards it. Then the magician picks up any two cards. The spectator chooses one of these and discards it.

The process continues until just one card is left. If it beats the ♠3, the spectator wins. Otherwise he loses.

The bet seems simple, honest and completely aboveboard. When the magician takes two cards from the deck the spectator can freely discard either one. When it is the magician's turn, he must withdraw one of the two cards offered to him by the spectator. Thus on every round the spectator is in complete control.

Needless to say, he loses.

METHOD: This ingenious force was devised by Roy Baker. The only preparation is lightly to pencil-dot or otherwise mark the back of the ♠2. With this card in the pack you can perform other tricks, since the marked ♠2 does not interfere with other stunts you may want to perform. When ready for "Speak of the Devil," proceed as follows.

Remove the 13 spades from the deck. Explain the bet. Then place the ♠3 aside, face up. Remark that the ace is low, the king is high.

The remaining 12 spades are mixed face down. The spectator goes first. He takes any two face-down cards. You choose one and discard it. Always choose a card that is not pencil-dotted. Discard that card. The other card goes back onto the pile.

Then it is your turn. Pick up two unmarked cards. The spectator chooses one of these and discards it. The remaining card goes back onto the pile.

Continue in this way, always following the simple rule. When the spectator offers you a choice of either of his two cards, pick the unmarked card. When you take two cards from the pile and offer the spectator a choice, take two unmarked cards.

At the finish there will be only two cards left. One will be marked. This card is the ♠2. The spectator offers you a choice of either card. Naturally you choose the unmarked card. This leaves him with the ♠2 and he loses.

The trick may be expanded. If there are two force cards, either of which is equally acceptable (two deuces, for example, if you are doing a variation of the above trick) then mark both cards. At the finish there will be two cards left. Give the spectator a choice of discarding either card. Of course he must then be left with one of the force cards.

The approach works just as well with objects other than cards. Put blank pieces of paper in each of 12 envelopes or matchboxes. Put a $5 bill in the remaining envelope or matchbox and secretly mark this container. The spectator mixes the containers. Twelve of them are discarded, leaving just one *for you.* The spectator gets to keep the contents of the other 12. He gets 12 pieces of paper and you get the $5 bill.

59   THE STAPLED CARD

After you become acquainted with different force techniques, you can choose a method that is exactly appropriate to the trick you want to perform. One example will be given here, an application of the X-Force described in the opening pages of this chapter. Although the method is simple, the effect is spectacular.

As seen by the audience, the spectator chooses a card and signs the face. The card is returned to the deck. Then two jokers are shown. They are stapled together and placed on the bottom of the deck.

The magician causes one joker to come free of the staple. This is not a particularly magical effect, but then he causes the signed chosen card to become instantly stapled to the other joker!

METHOD: This is a streamlined handling of an intriguing plot idea suggested by Joseph Prieto. Two different approaches will be described here. You will need four jokers, a stapler and about a minute to set up the trick. Begin by stapling one joker back to back with the ♦3 as shown in Figure 52.

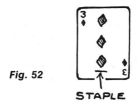

Fig. 52

STAPLE

Then staple one of the other jokers at the bottom and remove the staple. You want staple holes to mark this joker, so that later it will appear that this joker was magically released from the staple; that's why you first staple this joker and then remove the staple.

Hold the deck face up in the left hand. Place the three jokers on the top or back of the deck. The joker with the staple holes is third from the top. Place the ♦ 3–joker stapled pair at the face of the deck with the ♦ 3 showing. The setup is shown in Figure 53. This apparatus can be carried in the pocket until ready to perform. The extra cards can be added to the deck in just a few seconds when you are in another room.

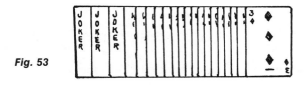

Fig. 53

To perform the routine, place the deck face down on the table. Have the spectator cut off half and place this half on the table. Place the other half on top, but crosswise, so that the stapled end of the packet is on top of the other half of the deck. This is the X-Force. Grasp the crossed packets as shown in Figure 54.

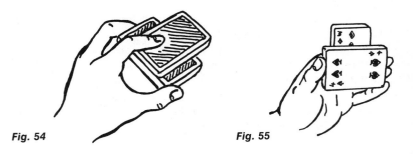

Fig. 54   *Fig. 55*

Turn the left hand palm up, Figure 55, to show the spectator that he cut to the ♦3. With the cards held exactly as shown in Figure 55, have the spectator sign his name on the face of the ♦3. Note that the lower packet hides the staple in the ♦3.

Place the deck face down on the table and square the cards. The signed ♦3 is now buried in the center of the deck. Remove the stapler from the pocket and place it on the table. Pick up the deck and fan it so you can see the faces. Remark that you will need two jokers for this effect. Cut the deck and complete the cut so that the stapled ♦3 is again on the bottom. Without showing the face of the ♦3 to the audience, place the deck face down on the table. Remove the top two cards and turn them face up to show they are jokers.

Place them back to back and staple them at one end. Try to have the staple in the same position on the jokers as it is on the ♦3. When the jokers have been stapled together, hold them in one hand and the deck in the other.

Say, "I could put these stapled jokers into the deck right next to your card without looking." As you say this put both hands behind the back. Immediately tuck the stapled jokers under the belt and leave them there. Take the stapled pair of cards off the bottom of the deck. This pair consists of the ♦3 and a joker. Hold them in the hand so that the joker is uppermost.

Bring the hands out into view again. It appears as if nothing has changed. The deck is in one hand and the two stapled cards are in the other. There is a joker showing at the top or face of the stapled pair, so the audience assumes the hand holds the two stapled jokers (see Figure 56). As you bring the cards back into view, say, "That is more easily said than done. Let me try something else."

Fig. 56

Place the deck on the table. Ask a spectator to hold his right hand palm up. Place the stapled pair of cards onto his palm. Have him cover the cards with his left hand palm down. Remove the top card of the deck. Don't show its face (it is a joker). Slide it between his palms, pause for dramatic effect, then abruptly pull this card out and turn it face up. It is a joker.

"It's easy to pull one joker free of the staple," you say. "The hard part is to cause your signed card to become stapled to the other joker."

The spectator opens his hands and finds that his signed card has somehow become stapled to the joker!

If you have access to double-sided adhesive tape, there is no need for duplicate cards. Any deck may be used. Place the two jokers that normally come with most decks on top. Double-sided tape has the adhesive on both sides, and is available in stationery and hardware stores. Cut a quarter-inch of clear double-sided tape and fasten it to the back of the top card of the deck. This card is a joker and there is a joker directly below it.

This is the only preparation. Hold the deck from above with the right hand. The left hand removes cards one at a time from the bottom until the spectator calls stop. Hand him the stopped-at card and tell him to sign the face. When he's done this, place his card face down on top of the deck. Cut the deck and complete the cut. Press down on the deck to make sure his card adheres to the joker that has the tape on top.

Bring the stapler out as you remark that you're going to use two jokers for the trick. Turn the deck face up, run through the cards and cut the two jokers to the bottom or face of the deck.

Remove them and place them face up in the left hand. Because of the adhesive tape, the chosen card adheres to the backmost joker. Take the face joker with the right hand, turn it face down and place it behind the double card in the left hand. When this joker is back to back with the double card, staple the two jokers together. Turn the stapled packet over so that the double card is at the bottom. Place the deck face down on top of the stapled cards.

Say, "That's how most people staple two cards together. A magician wouldn't bother with that method." Grasp the deck from the above with the right hand. The left hand grasps the bottom card of the deck and pulls it free of the staple. Toss this joker out face up on the table.

"Magicians staple cards together without the stapler." Cut the deck and complete the cut. Snap the fingers and spread the deck to reveal a face-up joker in the center. The spectator removes this card and will be surprised to discover that there is a card stapled back to back with it, and further, that this card is the signed chosen card.

TELEPATHY WITH CARDS

"Tricks dependent on thought foretold or divined are unquestionably the most striking in the whole range of conjuring. In truth, how is it possible to explain how anyone can know what you have chosen to think of, or even what you are going to think of presently?"

The above comment, written by Robert-Houdin a century ago, is as true today as when he practiced magic. Mental magic is almost always accepted as real magic by laymen. Properly presented, feats of mind reading with cards (or other objects) seem to lie beyond rational explanation. This chapter and a later one, "Thought-Card Methods," consider a number of telepathic experiments with cards.

60   THE PREDICTION DECK

The magician opens an envelope and takes out a deck of cards, explaining that the deck was mailed to him by an Oriental. In the deck, he says, is a prediction, fortunately written in English. It involves an event that has not yet taken place.

The pack is placed face down on the table. The spectator is invited to lift off less than half the deck. He can take one card or 25. The choice is entirely his and he is encouraged to try and second-guess the prophet by taking fewer or more cards than might be expected. After he takes some cards, he turns this packet face up and places it on the table.

When he has done this, have him place about half the remainder of the deck face down on top of the tabled face-up portion. The number of cards is not important as long as it contains the prediction slip.

Then have him turn the remainder of the deck face up and place it on top of the rest. At this point you have a face-up portion on top, then a face-down portion, then another face-up portion. No one has any idea of how many face-up cards and face-down cards there are.

Tell the spectator to lift off all the cards above the prediction. Then have him place the prediction aside without looking at the writing. Finally have him take the portion that was above the prediction, turn it over, and shuffle it into the balance of the deck. He can give the deck two or three more shuffles if he likes. The shuffles should be riffle shuffles.

Finally, have him count the number of face-down cards in the deck. He will arrive at a total of 24 face-down cards, exactly matching the prediction.

Note that you never touch the deck, yet the prediction is always correct.

METHOD: On a business card or square of cardboard write, "You will have exactly 24 face-down cards." Place the prediction, writing-side down, between the twenty-eighth and twenty-ninth cards from the top of the deck. Proceed as written above and the prediction will be correct. The routine is based on an idea of Bob Hummer's.

To add an exotic note, write your name and address on an airmail envelope and mail the empty envelope to yourself. Slide out the flap, place the deck with the prediction inside, and seal the flap. It will appear as if the deck was mailed to you. Remark that you have a mystic friend in the Far East who is good at writing predictions. Tear open the envelope, remove the deck and proceed as described above.

61 LAST OCTOBER

A deck of playing cards can act as a time-keeping device. On a slip of paper the magician writes, "October 21," explaining that this is the date of the first and only time he attempted this strange experiment with cards.

"Let me show you," he says. "October has 31 days. Please count 31 cards off the top of the deck." After the spectator does this, he discards the rest of the pack.

"Cut off a small packet of cards, count them and place them in your pocket," the magician says. The spectator secretly removes a small number of cards and pockets them. Say he has six cards. Only he knows this.

"Shuffle the rest of the packet. Then turn the top card face up on the table and sign your name on it." After the spectator has completed these instructions the magician adds, "Turn your signed card face down on the table. However many cards you have in your pocket, deal that many cards from the packet onto your signed card."

In our example the spectator deals six cards onto his signed card. After he has done this, he takes the small group of cards on the table (his signed card plus the six cards on top of it) and places this group on top of the packet in his hand. His chosen card is now buried somewhere in the packet.

"Since you have some cards in your pocket," the magician says, "I can't possibly know how many cards you have in your hand. That's what makes this so strange an experiment."

Turning attention to the date on the slip of paper, he says, "Before we started I wrote this date, October 21st. It happens that October is the tenth month. Count ten cards, moving each from the top to the bottom of your packet."

After the spectator has done this the magician says, "The date is the 21st, so count 21 cards, moving each from the top to the bottom of your packet."

When the spectator has done this, the magician says, "Now we get to the strange part. I wrote that date before we began. It would have been impossible for me to know how many cards you put in your pocket. Please turn over the top card of the packet in your hand."

The spectator does and it is his signed card!

The trick works itself. Just follow the above instructions and the signed card will always end up on the top of the packet.

62 MENTAL RESCUE

This splendid mental effect was originated by L. Vosburgh Lyons. Two spectators are seated opposite each other at a table. Each takes five cards from the deck. Each person shuffles his cards, chooses one, and places it in the other person's packet. The packets are each shuffled again by the spectators.

Picking up a packet, the magician concentrates for a moment, then removes one card. Picking up the other packet, the magician again concentrates and then removes a card. It turns out that these are the actual cards chosen by the two spectators.

METHOD: On top of the deck have five cards that you can easily memorize. The best plan when starting out is to use five digits in order from your telephone number and assign a suit to each. For the purpose of this explanation we'll use the ♣A, ♥4, ♠7, ♦10, ♣K. Note that the values increase by three as you go from card to card. The suits are in club-hearts-spade-diamond rotation, with a final club at the end. Place these five cards in any order on top of the deck.

Place the deck face down on the table. Have a spectator cut off about half and place this half on the table. Pick up the remainder of the deck (the original bottom half) and place it on top, but crosswise in the manner of the X-Force illustrated in Figure 46.

Explain that you would like to perform the first mind-reading experiment devised to allow you to do sleight of hand by telepathy. Lift off the portion of the deck that lies on top and deal the top five cards to one spectator. Put this portion aside. Then deal the top five cards of the other portion to the second spectator. These five cards are the force cards.

Have each spectator mix his cards without looking at them. Then have each choose a card, remember it and place it in the other spectator's packet. When this has been done, have each person mix his five cards.

Take the first spectator's packet, fan it and look for the ♣A, ♥4, ♠7, ♦10 or ♣K. Remove this card and place it face down on the table. Then pick up the second spectator's packet and look for the one card that does not belong with the force cards in that packet. The packet might contain the ♠7, ♥2, ♦10, ♣A and ♣K, in which case the card that doesn't belong to the force group is the ♥2. Remove this card and place it face down on the table.

Have the two chosen cards named. Then turn over the two cards you removed to show that you correctly found the two chosen cards.

Regarding presentation, after the cards have been chosen, exchanged and placed in opposite packets, have the packets shuffled, then ask each spectator to try and guess which card in his packet belongs to the other fellow. The difficulty of the problem becomes immediately apparent because neither spectator has a clue as to which card was chosen by the other spectator.

Another point is this. When you are going to find the chosen cards, take the second spectator's packet. This is the one containing four force cards plus the first spectator's card. Look through this packet, locate the card that doesn't belong to the force group, and place it face down on the table. But then look through the packet again and see which card is missing from the force group. In the above example the ♥4 is missing, and this is the second spectator's card. Thus you know his card *without* going near the other packet.

63   PAST AND FUTURE

The most impressive and memorable tricks are those that involve the spectator in a personal way. In this routine you predict the future by correctly foretelling which card a spectator is going to pick. Then you disclose the past by telling the spectator his date of birth.

The trick is impromptu. It uses no gimmicks or confederates.

METHOD: The basic idea is a routine of Verne Schoneck's. Use any borrowed deck and a paper bag. Take the deck and a pencil. Explain that you are going to write a prediction about an event in the future.

Lower the deck out of sight below the level of the tabletop. When the deck is out of the spectator's view, note the bottom card of the deck. Assume it's the ♠2. Remove the top card. On the face of this card write, "Two of spades." Place this card on the bottom of the deck face to face with the ♠2. Then remove the new top card, reverse it and place it on the bottom. The situation now is that there are two face-up cards on the bottom of the face-down deck. The third card from the bottom is the ♠2.

Remark that you'll put your prediction into the bag for safekeeping. Lower the deck into the bag and pretend to thumb off the prediction card into the bag. All you really do is rattle your hand a bit inside the bag.

Take the deck out of the bag. Remove the top card, toss it out face up and ask the spectator to write the month and day of his birth on the face of the card. Turn your head aside while he does this.

Have him place his card face down on top of the deck. Explain you want him to choose a card in a random way. Hand him the deck behind his back. As you do, secretly turn over the deck. Tell the spectator to take his card, reverse it and insert it into the deck. He follows your instruction, unaware he is actually inserting an indifferent card into the pack. After he has done this, have him cut the deck three times, and then turn it over three times.

He thinks his card is reversed somewhere in the deck. Take back the deck, turn it face up and spread it between your hands until you find the face-down card. Cut the deck and complete the cut so the reversed card is at the face of the deck. Remove this card and the card below it, explaining that the spectator's birthday card has found a card in a completely random way. Place both of these cards into the paper bag. Make it obvious you do not look at the face of the face-down card.

Now say that your first disclosure was a prediction about the future. Your next disclosure is more difficult because it's about the past. Place the deck below the level of the table. Note the writing on the top card. It will be the spectator's date of birth. Copy this date on another card and place this card on top of the face-down deck.

Say you will place your new card in the bag. As soon as the hand holding the deck goes into the bag and is hidden from view, thumb off the top two cards, letting them fall into the bag.

To finish, the spectator dumps out the contents of the bag, four cards in all. Two of the cards will be his, the other two yours. It is found that you successfully predicted the card he would choose, and then you disclosed his exact date of birth.

64 HOUDINI'S SECRET

This is a streamlined handling of a double prediction that appears in the Houdini notebooks. Before performing the trick, place a pencil dot at diagonally opposite corners of the top card of the deck, as in Figure 57. The dots should be large enough for you to spot easily but not so large as to make their presence obvious to the audience.

Fig. 57

The only other preparation is to note and remember the sixth card from the top of the deck. Assume this card is the ♥2. At the start of the trick you will thus have the pencil-dotted card on top of the deck and the ♥2 in position sixth from the top.

Tell the first spectator that you want him to think of a number and to deal that many cards off the top. "For example," you say, "If you thought of five, you would deal five cards like this." As you patter, deal five cards off the top into a heap on the table. Say, "Then look at the top card of the ones you dealt and drop the deck on top to bury your card." As you patter, glance at the top card of the dealt packet, place it back on top of that packet, and drop the balance of the deck on top of all.

Say, "Are you thinking of a number?" The spectator says yes. Lift off about half the deck from above with the right hand and remove the face card of this packet with the left fingers, as in Figure 58. Then replace the cut-off packet on top. Take the card removed with the left fingers, turn it face up and on it write, "Two of hearts." Place this card face down on the table.

Fig. 58

While you turn your back the spectator deals any number of cards between two and 12 onto the table, looks at the last card he dealt, and drops the balance of the deck on top of this card to bury it in the pack.

Face the spectators again. Cut off about two-thirds of the deck and complete the cut. You want to cut slightly fewer than 40 cards because your pencil-dotted key card is somewhere in the bottom 12 cards and you want to leave it undisturbed.

Turn to a second spectator. Say to him, "I want you to do the same thing. Deal cards like this." Here you deal single cards off the top into a tabled heap until you deal the pencil-dotted key card. Deal one more card. Say, "After you have dealt the cards, I want you to look at the last card dealt, like this." Glimpse the face of the last card you dealt. This is important because the card is the one chosen by the first spectator. Assume it is the ♠7.

Drop the deck on top of the dealt packet. Then lift off about half the deck with the right hand and take the face card, as in Figure 58. Glimpse the face of this card, say, "I want a card with more white space to write on," and put this card on top of the right-hand packet. Then take a new card with the left fingers. Drop the right-hand cards on top of the balance of the deck.

On the face of this card write the name of the card chosen by the first spectator. In our example you would write, "Seven of spades," the name of the card you glimpsed. Place the prediction on the table, writing side down.

Turn your back. Have the second spectator deal the same number of cards as the first spectator. He notes the last card dealt (it will be the force card, the ♥2 in our example), and drops the deck on top to bury his card.

Have the two cards named. Then have the predictions read to reveal that you knew all along which cards would be chosen.

This is a clever mental mystery that never fails to impress laymen.

65   HEX SQUARED

Shortly after its appearance in print, this routine was featured in a television show devoted to mental magic and was reprinted in a nationally distributed news weekly. To describe the effect is also to describe the method so we shall proceed immediately into the details. Arrange 16 cards in the color sequence indicated in Figure 59. The actual values and suits are of no consequence so long as the colors agree with the layout. Assuming the deck is red-backed, the card shown in the third column as the ♥A would be blue-backed. If the odd-color ♥A is not handy, draw a large X on the back of the ♥A in the deck you are going to use. Arrange the cards in the layout with the deck face up so that the X on the back of the ♥A is not seen by the audience.

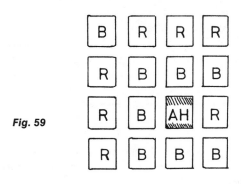

Fig. 59

After the cards are arranged in the face-up array, have the spectator use a ring or a coin as a marker. Caution him that he is not to study the cards or fix his attention on any card in the layout. Stress that he must act entirely on impulse in response to each command you give him.

To begin, tell him to place the ring on any red card in the layout. There are no restrictions. Emphasize that he must not hestitate in his choice. The card must be chosen on impulse.

Next tell him to move the ring either to the left or right to the nearest black card. Again there are no restrictions. He can move either to the left or right as long as he comes to rest on the black card nearest his starting position.

Now tell him to move vertically up or down to the nearest red card. Again stress that the move must be made without hesitation. In some rows he will have a wide degree of movement, in others he won't. In either case he is to move the ring without pause.

For the third move he is to move diagonally to the nearest black card. Again in some cases he is restricted, in others he is not.

There is one final instruction and this one is specific. Tell him to move the ring either down (toward himself) or to the right, in either case to the nearest red card.

All looks fair. The spectator has been given an unlimited choice in the way he may move, yet each move draws him deeper into a trap. If the above instructions are carried out correctly, the ring will now rest on the ♥A. To finish the trick, turn each card face down on the table until all cards in the layout are face down except the chosen card. Emphasize that the spectator had complete freedom of choice on each move, that he could slide the ring any way he chose. Then say that Fate nevertheless exercised a guiding hand. Turn over the ♥A to reveal that it has a different-color back.

In order for the trick to work, the layout of Figure 59 must be as the spectator sees it, not as the magician sees it.

66   THE SQUARE RING

This version of "Hex Squared" uses only three instructions to the spectator. As before, the spectator slides a coin or a ring over an array of cards in response to three directions from the magician. It is then shown that the magician knew all along which card would be chosen. This version was developed by Sam Schwartz and the author.

Because only three instructions are given to the spectator, he will not always end up on the same card. There are in fact two cards he can end up on. They are accounted for by means of two "outs" (alternate endings) used by the magician.

The array is shown in Figure 60. The ♥A has a back colored differently than the other cards.

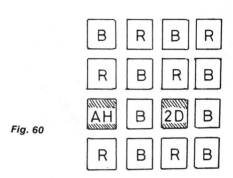

Fig. 60

On a square of cardboard write the following instructions:
1. Slide the coin up or down to the nearest red card.
2. Slide the coin left or right to the nearest black card.
3. Slide the coin diagonally to the nearest red card.

On the back of this card write the words, "You will choose the ♦2." This completes the prior preparation. The entire outfit may be placed in an envelope and carried in the pocket. When ready to perform this routine, remove the cards and the cardboard square, saying that these particular cards seem to exert a psychic influence on certain mental wavelengths.

To present the routine, deal out 16 cards in the array of Figure 60. The cards must be dealt out face up from the face-up deck to conceal the odd-color back of the ♥A.

Place the cardboard square on the table with the instructions up. Do not let the audience see the writing on the back of the cardboard. Have the spectator remove a coin from his pocket. Instruct him to place it on any black card. Emphasize that the cards and the cardboard square are the *only* apparatus you will use.

Have the spectator slide the coin according to the three instructions described above. If the coin ends up on the ♥A, turn over the other 15 cards, then the ♥A to show the odd-color back. If the coin ends up on the ♦2, turn over the cardboard square to show the written prediction. The coin can end up on only one of these two cards, so all possible outcomes have been accounted for.

67   THE UNMATCH GAME

In this game the magician correctly predicts the outcome, then issues a second prediction and is correct once again.

Ten pairs of cards are arranged so that suits match up. A sample arrangement might be a pair of spades, a pair of hearts, a pair of clubs, a pair of spades, a pair of diamonds and so on. On top of these ten pairs of cards place a heart, a spade, a diamond and a club. Place this packet of 24 cards on top of the deck and you are ready to begin.

To present the routine, remove the top 24 cards. Discard the rest of the deck as it will not be used. Give the packet to the spectator and let him shuffle it thoroughly. While the spectator shuffles the cards, you write on a slip of paper, "There will be exactly four cards left over, and there will also be just one of each suit." Fold the paper and place it in plain view on the table.

Have the spectator place the shuffled packet face down on the table. Then ask him to divide it into two *unequal* heaps with any number of cards in each heap. He keeps one heap for himself and gives the other to a second spectator.

The game is to fan the cards out and remove any pair of the same suit. Place the pair face down on the table and keep removing matching-suit pairs until he has no more matching pairs. The second spectator similarly does this with the cards in his packet. Remark, "If for instance you have two Hearts, place them on the table. Then two clubs, two diamonds, and so on."

When they have done this, they will be left with a number of unmatched cards. The prediction is then opened and read aloud. There are indeed just four cards left unmatched, and they are one of each suit.

Offer to repeat the trick. Take the four cards from them and drop them onto the balance of the deck or put them in the pocket since they are not used. Pick up the matching pairs on the table (ten pairs in all) and hand them to one of the spectators. Ask him to shuffle them thoroughly.

While the cards are being shuffled, write, "The first spectator will have exactly the same number of cards remaining as the second spectator. In addition, the suits of the first spectator's remaining cards will be exactly the same as the suits in the second spectator's remaining cards."

Again the spectators remove matching-suit pairs (two hearts, two clubs, etc.) from their respective packets until they can go no further. The remaining cards are compared with the prediction and it is seen that, once again, the prediction is correct.

There is a slight chance that all cards will be perfectly matched up, but the prediction is still correct. The above routine is based on ideas of Roy Walton and the author.

68 THE MASTER MIND

The magician removes a deck from his pocket and deals cards off the face one at a time. The spectator can call stop at any time. There is no force and every card is different. The spectator chooses any card. This card is buried in the deck. No one knows where the card is in the pack. This pack is then returned to the jacket pocket.

Another deck is brought from a different jacket pocket. The magician says, "Before I came here tonight I reversed a card in this deck." He spreads the pack face up and it is seen that one card is face down. This card is pushed out of the deck.

"Your card was the eight of clubs," the magician says. "Wouldn't it be amazing if the card I reversed was also the eight of clubs?" The reversed card is turned over and it is indeed the ♣8!

"Not only that," the magician adds, "But I was so sure you'd pick the ♣8 I put another one in the deck." He spreads the deck to reveal that there is another ♣8 in the pack.

Tapping the ♣8 in the deck, the magician says, "But *this* eight of clubs belongs here." He flips the deck over to show it is blue-backed.

"*Your* eight of clubs doesn't." Now the ♣8 on the table is flipped over. It has a red back. The spectator picked the only red-backed card in the deck!

All may be left with the spectator for examination.

METHOD: This is a streamlined version of an effect whose originator is unknown to me. It can be done with two regular decks but you may find the working a little easier if you use the smaller novelty decks which are half the size of regular playing cards. The small decks are available in novelty and gift shops. In a moment you will see why the smaller decks are more convenient.

Two decks are needed, one red-backed and one blue-backed.

After shuffling the red-backed deck take the top 26 cards. Assume the ♠A is at the face or bottom of this packet.
Remove the same 26 cards from the blue-backed deck, shuffle them and place this packet face down on the table. Place a blue-backed joker face down on top of the packet. Then place a red-backed joker face up on the packet. Finally, place the 26-card red-backed packet face up on top of all. The ♠A will be on top at this point. Snap a rubber band around this deck and place it in your right jacket pocket. The rest of the blue-backed deck is in the left jacket pocket. Place a pencil in the right pocket. You are ready to begin.

Remove the banded deck from the pocket with the ♠A uppermost. Take the rubber band off the deck and place the band in the right jacket pocket. Hold the deck in the left hand. The ♠A shows at the face of the deck.

Deal the cards one at a time onto the table in a face-up heap. Tell the spectator to stop you at any time. Of course he must stop you somewhere in the first 26 cards. When he does, have him remember the card he stopped at. Keep this card face up. Insert it face up into the deck about 13 cards up from the bottom. Thus the card enters the blue-backed portion of the deck.

Gather the dealt cards and replace them face up on top of the deck. Then snap the rubber band around the deck. Keep this face of the deck toward the spectator as you place the deck into your *inside* left jacket pocket with the right hand.

The crucial action takes place at this point. The deck does not go into the pocket. It goes into the left jacket sleeve. The right hand comes out of the jacket so that the spectator can clearly see that the hand is empty. The left hand then goes to the left (side) pocket to remove another deck. Actually the deck just dropped into the sleeve tumbles down the sleeve and into the left hand and it is *this same deck* that is brought out of the left pocket. The deck is brought out with the blue-backed packet uppermost. The deck appears to be face up.

Remark that yesterday you had a sudden thought that someone was going to choose a particular card and that you reversed one card in this deck. Spread the facemost 26 cards between the hands, revealing a face-down card in the middle of the face-up group. Be careful not to spread past the joker.

The right hand removes all of the face-up cards except the joker and spreads them face up on the table. All attention is on that single face-down card in the middle of the spread. Both hands go to the jacket pockets as you remark that you will need a pencil. The left hand drops its packet (a red-backed packet plus two jokers) into the left pocket and comes out with the balance of the blue-backed deck. At the same time the right hand comes out of the right pocket with the pencil. To focus attention on the right hand, look at the pencil as it is being removed from the pocket.

Use the eraser end of the pencil to slide the face-down card out of the spread as you say, "I don't want this card touched by human hands. You might think I switched cards."

Have the spectator turn the card over. It is the same as his freely chosen card. After this has registered with the spectator, use the pencil to point to the duplicate in the face-up spread. Finally, gather the complete deck (tabled cards plus the cards in the left hand) and flip the deck face down, revealing blue backs. The spectator chose the only red-backed card in a blue-backed deck.

It should be obvious that if you use the smaller decks, the cards will slide down the jacket sleeve more easily. Try it with regular cards also. If it works, stick to those cards. Otherwise use the smaller decks.

GAMBLING SECRETS

Almost everyone has played cards, even if only the occasional game of Old Maid or Go Fish, and has probably wished for the ability to deal himself a winning hand. Gambling demonstrations are always popular because they satisfy the dream of being able to control a deck of cards.

If you can deal any hand called for, demonstrate your prowess at a classic swindle like Three-Card Monte or produce the aces, you will have impressed your audience with a demonstration of uncanny skill. These feats and others will be explained in this chapter.

69   FLIM FLAM

In this quick demonstration of skill at Seven-Card Stud Poker you deal a face-down heap of seven black cards and a separate face-down heap of seven red cards. Don't show the audience the faces of the cards as you remove them from the deck. Place one heap on top of the other.

Hold the face-down packet from above in the right hand. The left thumb draws the top card off. Simultaneously the left fingers draw the bottom card off, in Figure 61. Explain that you will draw pairs of cards off like this and that at some point the spectator is to call stop.

Fig. 61

Drop the first pair of cards onto the table. Draw off the next pair. If the spectator doesn't call stop, drop this pair onto the first pair. Continue drawing pairs of cards and dropping them onto the tabled pairs until the spectator calls stop. Whatever pair of cards you are holding in the left hand at this point, turn the two cards over as a unit, remarking that these will be the hole cards in two stud-poker hands. Leave them face up and drop them onto the tabled pairs of cards.

Continue drawing pairs of face-down cards off until all seven pairs have been dropped onto the tabled heap. Square up the cards. Invite the spectator to cut the packet and complete the cut. He can give the packet any number of straight cuts. Just make sure the face-up cards are in the middle of the packet before proceeding.

Deal the cards into two hands of seven-card stud poker. The face-up card in each hand is the hole card.

Say, "I'm not going to switch the hole cards. That would be too easy. Instead I'm going to switch all the other cards in each hand." Snap your fingers over the cards. Then point to the face-up black card, saying, "This card is black, but now all the others are red." Turn over this hand to show that the face-up black card is the only black card in the hand. The other cards are red.

Point to the face-up red card. Say, "This card is red, but now all the other cards in the hand are black." Turn over the hand to show that the face-up red card is the only red card in the hand. All the other cards are black.

70 MONTE MIRACLE

Three-Card Monte is a fair-seeming game that requires sleight-of-hand ability and a quick tongue to demonstrate successfully, but there is a version that uses a puzzling optical illusion to bring about the basic effect. As in the classic trick, you use two black cards and a red ace. The spectator is asked to guess the whereabouts of the ace. Although the ace is prominently placed, the spectator fails to find it.

Use the two black deuces and the ♥A. Place the ace between the deuces, but at right angles, as in Figure 62. Grasp the leftmost two cards with the left hand from above, and the rightmost deuce with the right hand as shown in Figure 63.

Turn the left hand palm up to show that the ♥A is at right angles to the other card. Then slip the two face-up cards under the

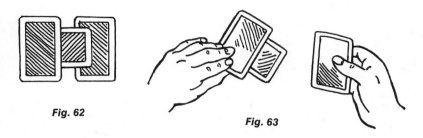

Fig. 62

Fig. 63

right thumb, as in Figure 64. The left hand then releases its grip on these two cards and regrips the two face-up cards with the fingers on top, thumb below. The grip is shown in Figure 65A.

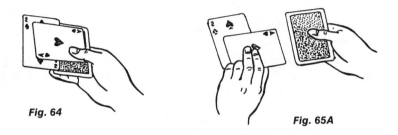

Fig. 64

Fig. 65A

Both hands now turn over simultaneously. The left-hand cards are face down and the right-hand card is face up, as in Figure 65B. As you do this, say, "And here is the other black deuce," calling attention to the black deuce in the right hand.

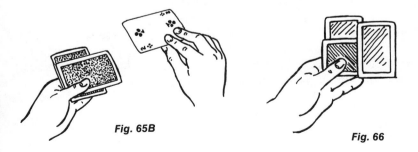

Fig. 65B

Fig. 66

Turn the right hand palm down and place the right-hand card on top of the left-hand cards as shown in Figure 66. There is one card between two others, and this card is at right angles to the other two cards. The audience assumes this is the red ace, but when you turn it over, it is not an ace.

71 WHIZ BANG POKER

One of the most difficult poker deals is to deal any number of hands from two to six, guarantee that each hand is a good hand and, finally, give the dealer the best hand of all. T. Nelson Downs devised an excellent method requiring no skill.

From two to six hands may be dealt. The top part of the deck is stacked. The setup from the top down is as follows: ♠J-♣7-♦8-♦9-♠10-♥6-♥7-♣8-♠9-♦10-♠6-♦7-♥8-♣9-♥10-♦6-♠7-♠8-♥9-♣10-♥J-♦A-♠2-♥4-♥3-♣6-♦Q-♦5-♠4-♥5-♥A.

Ask the spectator how many hands are to be dealt. If he says two, remark, "That's ten cards." Deal off a packet of ten cards into a heap on the table, reversing their order as you deal them into a face-down heap. Pick up this packet and deal two hands. Each hand is a straight, but yours is the winning hand.

If three hands are called for, say, "That's 15 cards," and deal a packet of 15 cards into a face-down heap. Then deal out three hands from the 15-card packet. Again you will get the winning hand.

If four hands are called for, say, "That's 20 cards," deal off 20 cards into a packet, then deal out four hands from this packet. Again all hands will be pat hands and you will have the winning hand.

If five hands are called for, *don't* reverse count the cards. Simply deal out five poker hands. You will get four tens, a winning hand.

Finally, if six hands are called for, bury the top card of the deck on the bottom of the deck, then count 30 cards into a packet, and then deal out six hands from this packet. The players will get straights and flushes but you will get a straight flush, the winning hand. As Downs himself remarked, "Try this—it's a corker!"

72 ANY HAND CALLED FOR

In the T. Nelson Downs poker deal, the magician dealt any number of hands and always came up with the winning hand. Here Michael Zens varies the plot by having the spectator name any kind of hand (royal flush, four of a kind, etc.). The magician deals the cards, turns up the dealer's hand, and it is the very hand named by the spectator. This is an impressive demonstration of skill at the card table.

By means of ingenious thinking, complicated setups are done away with. The Zens stack is ♥10-♥J-♥K-♥Q-♥A— ♠A-♠K-♦A-♣A-♣K, from the top down. Place this packet on top of the deck.

Ask for any poker hand. If the spectator names a straight, a straight flush or a royal flush, proceed directly into the deal described below by dealing out five hands, then gathering the hands one on top of the next, and then dealing out five hands again. The dealer's hand will contain the straight, the straight flush or the royal flush.

If the spectator asks for one pair, take one card from the top of the deck and bury it in the center of the pack. If he calls for two pair, bury the top two cards in the center of the pack. If he asks for three of a kind, bury the top three cards in the center. If he asks for four of a kind, bury the top four cards in the center. Finally, if he asks for a full house, bury the top five cards in the center of the deck.

When this has been done, deal out five face-down poker hands of five cards each. Deal from left to right, a card at a time, until you have five Draw Poker hands. As you deal, say, "This is how the honest gambler deals out poker hands. You don't see too many honest dealers these days." You can even show one or two hands to be worthless.

Gather the hands by placing the hands on top of one another until all five hands have been gathered and placed on top of the deck. Then deal out five hands again as you say, "This is how the card cheat deals poker hands."

Remind the spectator which hand he called out. Then turn over your hand to show that you dealt yourself the very hand called out by the spectator.

Note that in most cases the spectator will ask you to deal a royal flush and that you can proceed immediately into the deal with no adjustment in the cards.

73 THE OMEGA BET

Properly presented, this wager will establish your reputation as master of betting games. It begins as a simple game. When the spectator begins to get suspicious about the procedure you immediately tighten the conditions. When he gets more suspicious you tighten the conditions further. Should he still be suspicious (especially in view of your unbroken winning streak) you make it impossible for cheating to occur, yet you still win.

The game is simple and the cards are handled by the spectator from start to finish. Your only task is to watch the cards and see to it that the simple handling procedure is adhered to. This routine is the author's use of a riffle-shuffle set up in which a single card is "shuffled" into the deck by the spectator.

To establish the setup, arrange the cards so the colors alternate red-black-red-black from top to bottom. This is the only preparation. As the audience sees it, the spectator cuts the deck and completes the cut. Then he deals the top card and the next card face up onto the table. He chooses either card and inserts it face up anywhere in the deck. The spectator then deals the cards off the top in pairs, that is, two at a time. Sooner or later the pair containing the face-up card will show up. You bet whether the card paired with it will be the same color or not.

Since you win on every round, the spectator will eventually suspect that the color of the face-up card has something to do with it. When this proves wrong, he will suspect that you gauge the location of the face-up card in the deck. The real secret is much simpler. When he deals the top two cards onto the table, remember which one he dealt first. If he inserts that card face-up into the deck, it will pair up with a card of the same color, no matter where it goes into the deck. If he inserts the other card into the pack, it will not pair up with a card of matching color. This is *all* there is to it.

Knowing the system, you now proceed as follows with the routine. Tell him to cut the deck and complete the cut. He can give the deck any number of straight cuts. Then tell him to turn the top card face up onto the table. Say this is the ♥A. He then deals the next card face up alongside it. Say this card is the ♠4.

Have him choose either card and place it face up anywhere in the face-down deck. Say he decides to insert the ♥A face up in the deck. Since this is the first card he dealt off the top, it will pair up with a card of the same color. This means that both cards of the pair containing the face-up ♥A will be red.

Don't make the game look too easy. Before you say anything, glance at the ♠4 still on the table. Then glance at the deck. Pretend to make a mental calculation. Then announce that when the spectator deals the pair containing the face-up ♥A, both cards of that pair will be red.

The spectator pushes the top two cards off the deck and transfers them to the bottom. He does the same thing with the next pair and the next, continuing until he comes to the pair containing the face-up ♥A.

The card paired with the ♥A is turned face up. It will be red. You have won the wager.

The handling here is important. When the spectator acknowledges you won, have the ♥A dealt onto the table. The red card paired with the ♥A is then turned face down and returned to the top of the deck. Place the ♥A and the ♠4 aside as they are no longer used.

This same pattern of handling is repeated throughout the remainder of the demonstration. Have the spectator cut the deck and complete the cut, then turn the top two cards up, and so on. You should perform this phase of the Omega Bet several more times until the spectator begins to get suspicious. Sooner or later the spectator will tell you that the color of the face-up card must have something to do with it. He will reason that if you don't know the color of the card he inserts into the deck, you won't win quite as often.

When this happens, have him deal the top two cards face down onto the table so that no one can see the faces of the cards. He takes either card, places it behind his back, turns it face up and inserts it reversed into the face-down deck. Simply note whether he places the first card or the second card into the deck. If it's the first card, the colors will match. If it's the second card, the colors won't match.

Have him bring the deck forward, deal cards from top to bottom two at a time, and stop when he gets to the pair containing the face-up card. As before you will have correctly predicted whether the pair containing the face-up card will or won't contain two cards of the same color.

For the next phase of the routine, write on a slip of paper, "The cards won't match." Toss the paper out, writing-side down. Then have the spectator place the deck behind his back, cut the deck and complete the cut. With the cards still out of sight, he takes either the top card or the bottom card of the face-down deck, turns it face up and inserts it anywhere in the deck. The deck is brought forward.

Then he transfers pairs of cards from top to bottom until he comes to the pair containing the face-up card. This pair will contain one red card and one black card. The colors don't match, so your prediction is correct.

For the final phase, write on a piece of paper, "Each pair will match." Have the spectator put the deck behind his back. Tell him to cut the deck and complete the cut. Have him take the bottom card, turn it face up and insert it into the top half of the deck. Then have him take the top card, turn it face up and insert it face up into the bottom half of the deck.

The spectator brings the deck into view and deals cards off two at a time. Each pair containing a face-up card is placed aside. At the finish, when each of these two pairs is examined, it is seen that the predictions are correct—each pair does contain two cards of the same color.

74 ACES FOR EXPERTS

The production of the four aces is one of the most impressive feats you can perform with a deck of cards. The catch is that if you use a borrowed deck, with no time to set the cards, there is generally a great deal of technical skill called for if you want to produce the aces in a magical manner. The following routine was devised by the author as a streamlined ace production requiring no skill.

Taking a borrowed, shuffled deck, the magician holds the cards face up so that only he can see the faces. He first checks that the aces are evenly distributed throughout the pack. If two or more aces are bunched together, the deck is given a few shuffles to separate them. Then the deck is spread again. Spreading the cards from left to right, when he gets to the first ace he removes the card just to the left of it, turns it around and inserts it in its original position. This reversed card is left upjogged.

The same procedure is repeated with the card just to the left of each of the remaining three aces. The result is the situation shown from the performer's view in Figure 67.

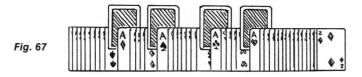

Fig. 67

The deck is squared up. The upjogged cards are carefully squared into the pack. Then the deck is turned over side for side and held in the left hand. All of the cards above the first reversed card are removed and placed on the bottom of the deck. The topmost face-up card is dealt onto the table. Then all of the cards above the next face-up card are taken and placed on the table below this first face-up card. Then the next face-up card is placed on the table. All of the cards above the next face-up card in the deck are placed on the table in a group below the second face-up card on the table.

The third face-up card is placed on the table. All of the face-down cards above the last face-up card in the deck are placed on the table in a group below the third face-up card. Finally, the fourth face-up card, which is now on top of the remainder of the deck, is dealt onto the table. The remaining face-down cards are placed on the table just below this card. The result looks like Figure 68.

Fig. 68

The four face-up cards are handed to the spectator with the remark that his gambling expertise is about to be tested. He is to mix the four cards and place each face-up card next to a face-down packet.

In the example of Figure 68 he may place the ♥5 next to the first packet on the left. Pick up this packet, spell "five," dealing a card for each letter into a heap and place the balance of the packet on top of the dealt cards. He might have placed the ♥4 next to the next packet. Pick up this packet, spell "four," dealing a card for each letter into a face-down heap, and drop the balance of the packet on top of the dealt cards.

Proceed in like manner for the remaining packets, using the deal-spell indicated by the value of the face-up card in front of the packet.

For the finish, turn over the packets to reveal the four aces at the face of the packets.

75   FACE-UP POKER

This chapter closes with a poker bet that is little known outside a small circle. The details of this ingenious bet have surfaced in various publications, but this is believed to be the first complete description of all angles on the proposition. The game assumes that the players have a knowledge of the way poker hands are ordered. From highest to lowest, the hands are rated as follows:

1. Royal flush	6. Straight
2. Straight flush	7. Three of a kind
3. Four of a kind	8. Two pair
4. Full house	9. One pair
5. Flush	10. High card

The game is this. The deck is shuffled and spread face up on the table. You are going to play two rounds. In the first round the spectator is allowed to go first. He may draw any five-card Draw Poker hand he likes. Everyone sees his cards. After he has drawn a hand, the magician draws a five-card hand.

Knowing what the magician has, the spectator has the option of keeping his hand or of discarding any part of it. He can discard one card or even all five cards, in which case he may draw a completely new hand. Once the spectator has exercised his option, the magician likewise can discard any part or all of his own hand and draw new cards.

Neither player can draw from the discard pile, and all suits rate equally. Although the player goes first and can draw any hand he likes, the magician bets that he can equal or better the spectator's hand. This means that the magician will either tie or beat the spectator on this round.

After the first round has been played, the second round goes like this. The magician goes first and can draw any five cards he likes. The spectator knows what the magician has and can draw any five cards he likes.

The magician then has the option of keeping his hand or of discarding up to five cards and drawing new cards from the balance of the deck. After he does this, the spectator has the option of discarding up to five cards from his hand and drawing new cards from the balance of the deck.

The difference in this round is that the magician goes first. But on this round he bets that he will positively beat the spectator. After the hands have been drawn it is seen that although the spectator knows how the magician has played on the first round and can utilize a similar strategy, the magician does indeed win on the second round.

We'll consider first-round play in detail. Almost always the spectator will draw a royal flush the first time. If he does this, you draw a royal flush too. The round ends in a tie.

Don't go on to the second round yet. Instead, point out that the game is more interesting if neither you nor the spectator draw a royal flush. Tell the spectator that by drawing some other hand, he will get a chance to see the strategy you use, and he can borrow from that strategy on the second round of play.

If the spectator agrees to this, chances are he will draw four aces and a king. This is the next highest hand after a straight flush, so it is to be expected that the spectator will draw this hand.

Should he draw four of a kind, you want to prevent him from improving the hand but at the same time you don't want to expose the strategy you intend to use on the second round. The approach you use is to draw three tens plus two more cards in the suit not included among the tens. The two cards can be any of these pairs: A-9, K-9, Q-9, J-9, K-8, Q-8, J-8, Q-7, J-7, J-6. This approach was suggested by Charles Foster and Christine Peipers.

For example, say the spectator draws the four aces plus the ♥K. You then draw the ♠10- ♦10-♣10 plus the ♥Q and ♥9. The spectator now has a chance to improve his hand but has trouble because you have blocked him from getting anything above a nine-high straight flush. If he draws, say, a nine-high straight flush in diamonds, you easily win with a ten-high straight flush in spades. You do this by discarding all but the ♠10, then draw the ♠9, ♠8, ♠7 and ♠6.

Second-round play is even easier. This time you draw *four* tens and any king. The best the spectator can do is settle for a nine-high straight flush. You easily beat him with a ten-high straight flush.

To summarize, on the first round you draw three tens plus two more cards. On the second round you draw four tens plus any king. The only way the spectator can beat you is if he knows the system.

There are two unpublished variations that the reader may want to consider. In the first, each player takes a turn and draws a single card out of the deck. Players alternate until each has five cards. The player with the highest hand wins.

A discussion of this game lies outside the scope of this book, but the reader may be interested in an amusing variation of the original bet, called Revenge Poker. Here the magician draws five cards, then the spectator draws five cards. Then the magician may discard and draw up to five new cards, and then the spectator may discard and draw up to five new cards. The difference is that each person draws cards for the *other* player. In other words, the magician draws the spectator's hand and the spectator draws the magician's hand.

The game gets its name from the fact that the spectator here can exercise revenge and give the magician the worst possible hand. If the magician ends up with a poker hand more awful than the spectator's hand, the magician loses.

The magician goes first. He draws four deuces and any other card. The spectator might just as well quit at this point, but since the cards drawn by the magician are for the spectator's poker hand, it appears as if the magician made a mistake since four of a kind represents an excellent hand.

The spectator will probably draw a three, four, five, six, eight, in mixed suits for the magician. This is a hand that contains an eight-high and nothing else. It is assumed that aces are higher than kings, in which case the hand drawn by the spectator for the magician represents the worst possible hand he can give the magician under the circumstances.

The magician holds onto one deuce, discards the rest of his hand, and then draws a three, four, five, seven. This hand becomes the spectator's hand. It is a truly awful hand and must lose for the spectator, no matter what cards he gives the magician. To say it another way, the worst the magician can get from the spectator is a hand with an eight as the highest possible card. The worst the magician can give the spectator is a seven-high hand. Since the spectator gets the lower hand, he loses.

CONJUROR'S QUARTET

This is a series of four quick tricks which use a variety of props that can be carried in the pocket, and require nothing special in the way of setting-up procedure. The props consist of a deck of cards, a die and two rubber bands. The other prop is an invisible confederate who helps out with one of the tricks.

The reader should find it easy to choose four or five tricks from the material presented in this book to make up his own personal card routine. The tricks in the present chapter might be used as a guideline. They are easy to perform, clear in plot and varied in both the type of effect and the props that are used.

76   INVISIBLE CON MAN

In this trick you require one visible spectator and one invisible spectator. A prediction is written and placed aside. You have a card noted by the throw of a die. The die then locates the chosen card, and for a kicker it locates a card that the invisible spectator would have chosen had he been present.

Before beginning the trick, note the top card of the deck. Say it is the ♠A. This small bit of preparation is done secretly. To perform the trick, remark that you wanted to include a friend of yours in the trick, a well-known con artist who frequently acts as your confederate, but he couldn't make it. "He did tell me, though, that he'd call as soon as he got out of jail." You further explain that he said that he'd pick a card anyway. The name of this card (the ♠A) is then jotted down on a slip of paper, which is placed aside.

Have the spectator deal two heaps of seven cards each. The heap which contains the ♠A at the bottom will be called A. The other heap will be called B. After he has dealt the two heaps, have him roll a die and note the top number. Whatever the number, he deals that many cards off the top of *B*, notes the face or bottom card of this dealt packet, and places the dealt packet on top of *A*. Then he places the combined packets at *A* on top of heap *B* and squares up the cards.

Have him deal seven cards into a heap on the table and place the balance of the cards aside. Turn the die over. Whatever number is up, deal that many cards off the top of the dealt packet. Turn up the next card and it will be his card. This completes the first part of the trick; the die has found his card.

Turn the die over again, bringing the original number uppermost. Deal that many cards off the top of the other packet and turn up the last card dealt. It will be the ♠A. Say, "Not only did the die find your card, it found the card my friend would have chosen had he been a free man." Have the spectator open the slip of paper and verify that the die did indeed locate a card chosen by the phantom spectator.

77   THE CALCULATOR CARD TRICK

This version of a classic swindle was proposed by J. W. Sarles. Explain that you have a deck of cards which has been programmed to act like a pocket calculator. It has the advantage that it requires no batteries and will never wear out.

Place the deck on your fingers. Have the spectator cut off about half and place the cut portion on your palm, Figure 69. In the drawing he would have cut off packet *A* and placed it on your palm. Turn up the top card of *B*. It might be an eight-spot.

Fig. 69

Say, "If I had 15 dollars and gave you eight [point to the eight-spot when you say this], how much money would I have left?"

The spectator answers, "Seven." Congratulate him on his being right. Then turn up the top card of packet *B* and it is a seven-spot!

The trick is immediately repeated and the calculator is once again correct.

METHOD: The only preparation is to note and remember the top card of the deck. In the above example this card is a seven-spot. Have the spectator cut off a packet of cards onto your palm. Then turn up the top card of packet *B*. Whatever its value, mentally add this to the card you memorized. In our example the top card of *B* is an eight, so you would silently add eight and seven, getting 15. Say to the spectator, "Suppose I had 15 dollars [here you name the total of the two numbers] and gave you eight [here you point to the eight-spot he cut to]. How much would I have left?" When he says, "Seven," simply turn up the top card of *A* to show it is a seven.

The trick is over so quickly that the spectator will ask you to do it again. J. W. Sarles devised this ending. Beforehand you note both the top card and the bottom card of the deck. Assume the bottom card is a three-spot.

Do the first part of the trick as described above. Then put packet *A* back on top of packet *B*. Say, "It works with other problems too. Here, cut the deck again." Once more the deck is placed on the fingers. The spectator cuts off a packet onto the left palm. Call this packet *A*.

Turn over packet *A*, bringing the face card of this packet into view. Whatever its value, add it to the value of the bottom card. If the face card of *A* is a nine, mentally add it to three, getting 12. Say, "Suppose I had 12 gallons of gas and I used nine gallons to get home. How much would I have left?"

The spectator answers three. Turn over the other packet, showing the three-spot at the face. Then put the deck aside, saying you don't want to burden the calculator with overuse.

78 BANDIT ACES

The four aces are removed from the deck and dealt out in a face-down row on the table. A rubber band is snapped around the rest of the deck for safekeeping. The spectator then names any ace. The four aces are placed on top of the banded deck. On command the named ace penetrates the deck.

METHOD: Remove the four aces from the deck and place them in a face-down row on the table in an order known to you. Assume they are from left to right, the ♣A, ♥A, ♠A, ♦A.

Snap a rubber band around the middle of the deck. The rubber band should fit snugly and it should be untangled.

Have any ace called out. Say the spectator names the ♥A. Drop the banded deck on top of the ♥A, as in Figure 70. Then pick up the deck plus the ♥A and place them on top of another ace. Pick up the deck plus the two aces and drop them on top of another ace. Finally drop the deck plus the three aces on top of the last ace. It makes no difference in which order the aces are picked up under the banded deck so long as the named ace is picked up first.

Fig. 70

The deck is on the table. The right hand grasps the deck from above, bears down on it and slides it to the right as in Figure 71. Three of the aces may spread a bit but the important point is that the ♥A will be secretly stolen under the deck.

Fig. 71

Square the packet of three aces and place them on top of the banded deck. The audience thinks this packet still contains the four aces. Grasp the deck from above with the right hand, using the same grip depicted in Figure 71. Command the named ace to penetrate the deck. Lift the deck with the right hand. There is now a face-down card on the table. When it is turned over it proves to be the named ace.

79   HOUDINI CARD

This clever card mystery was invented by Jack Avis. As the audience sees it, a card is chosen, initialed and returned to the deck.

A rubber band is then placed widthwise around the pack. Another rubber band is placed lengthwise around the pack. The chosen card is still in the deck and the deck is sealed on all sides by the rubber bands.

Nevertheless, when the deck is covered with a handkerchief, the chosen card instantly comes free of the doubly banded deck.

METHOD: Before proceeding, secretly mark the back of the top card of the deck. This card will act as a key card. Spread the pack and have any card chosen. Ask the spectator to sign his name on the face of the card. He then places his card on top of the deck, cuts the deck and completes the cut. Tell him to give the deck several straight cuts to lose his card further in the pack. Take the deck from him and locate the key card. Cut it to the top of the deck. The spectator's card is now on the bottom. The key card may be marked on the back as in the example of Figure 57 (page 94) so that it is easily spotted when you spread the deck face down. It is then a simple matter to cut it to the top of the pack.

You are now going to snap two rubber bands around the deck. Place one band widthwise around the deck, from *C* to *D* in Figure 72. A second rubber band is then snapped around the deck from *A* to *B* as shown in Figure 73. It is important to place the first band on widthwise and the second band lengthwise. Do not flash the face of the bottom card of the deck when the bands are snapped around the pack.

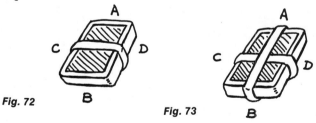

Fig. 72   **Fig. 73**

To remove the face card without disturbing the rubber bands, you will use a clever bit of handling that seems honest but is really the key to the method. Hold the deck in the left hand from above, as in Figure 74. The right forefinger moves to a position below the deck, presses against the face of the bottom card (the chosen card) and draws this card to the right, Figure 75A. As far as the audience is concerned, you are simply demonstrating the impossibility of withdrawing a card from the side of the pack. The right fingers tug on the card. As the card moves to the right the right thumb comes down on top of the card and helps pull it against the tension of the rubber band. As the card is drawn to the right, the rubber band will stretch. Release the bottom card and let it snap back square with the pack.

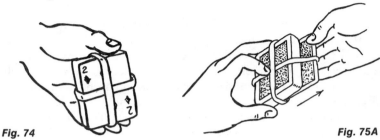

Fig. 74   **Fig. 75A**

Now grip the deck in the left hand as shown in Figure 75B. This time the right first finger takes the bottom card and pulls it forward a little over half its length. This action is shown in Figure 75B. The important point is that the lower end of this card will slip out from under the rubber band. When you allow the card to return, it will be *on top* of this band, as in an exposed view shown in Figure 76.

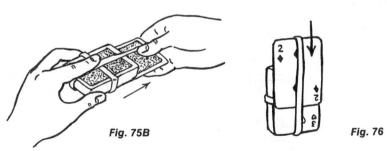

Fig. 75B   **Fig. 76**

Release this card, allowing it to snap back square with the deck. Then drop the deck face down on the table as you remove a handkerchief from your pocket. Cover the deck with the handkerchief. Then have a spectator hold the deck through the handkerchief. He holds the deck by the ends. Reach under the handkerchief, grasp the chosen card, then slide it out of the side of the deck and bring it out from under the handkerchief.

Ask for the name of the chosen card. Then turn over the card in hand to show that the signed card has somehow freed itself from the banded deck. All may be left with the spectator at this point.

THOUGHT-CARD METHODS

One of the most impressive tricks you can do with a deck of cards is to reveal a card merely thought of by the spectator. It is also one of the most difficult in a technical sense, requiring either special cards or sleight-of-hand ability. Still, there are a number of strictly self-working methods, and this chapter represents a survey of some of the best such approaches.

80 PSYCHORAMA

This ingenious trick was devised by Gene Grant and Sam Schwartz. The spectator is given a packet of five cards and is asked to think of one. By means of an elimination process the thought-of card is quickly discovered.

The five cards are chosen so that when the mentalist questions the spectator, he can expect to get not more than one "no" answer. By getting a series of "yes" answers, the mentalist makes it seem that he knows positively from the start which card was thought of.

The cards are the ♥9, ♦A, ♥K, ♣7 and ♥6. Remove them from the deck, mix them and hand them to the spectator. Turn your back and ask him to think of any one of the five cards.

When he has a card in mind, say, "A red card?" If he says no, the card is the ♣7. If he says yes, ask, "A Heart?" If he says no, the card must be the ♦A.

If he says yes, ask, "A spot card, wasn't it?" If he says no, it was the ♥K. If he says yes, ask, "Odd-valued, right?" If he says no, it was the ♥9. Otherwise it was the ♥6.

Note that as soon as you get a no answer, you positively know the thought-of card, and can name it immediately.

81   THOT-CARD MONTE

This is an offbeat method of revealing a thought-of card. The effect will vary from one performance to the next, so we shall detail the effect and method together.

Secretly place the ♠A on top of the deck, the ♠3 on the bottom and the ♠5 under your belt at the back of your trousers. Any three easily memorized cards may be used, but we will assume here that the above cards are employed in the trick.

Spread the deck face down on the table. Ask the spectator to remove the top card, a card from the middle, and the bottom card of the deck. Of course he will assume you know the top and bottom cards, but you don't know the card he takes from the middle. It can be any card.

Turn your back. Ask him to peek at one of these three cards and remember it. When he has done this, turn around and face him again. Place the ace on top of the middle card and place both of these on top of the ♠3. Remark that even if you know one or two of the cards, or even all three, you still don't know which card he chose.

Place the packet behind your back, saying that you will reverse one card. When the cards are out of sight remove the ♠5 from under the belt and place it on top of the packet. Then place the bottom card (♠3) under the belt.

Finally, turn the bottom card face up. You won't know which card this is because it came from the middle of the pack. Bring the packet into view and spread the cards to show the face-up card.

Say, "You didn't choose this card, did you?" If the spectator chose that card, the trick is over. Generally he will telegraph this fact by smiling or exclaiming when you spread the cards.

In the more likely case he will say no. Nod and say, "I thought so. And you didn't pick this card either. Turn the ♠5 face up. Of course the spectator could not have chosen this card because it was under your belt when he selected a card.

At this point the situation is as shown in Figure 77. The spectator assumes that the center card is his card but this is not necessarily true. He could have chosen the card behind your back. The ambiguity is cleared up in a subtle way.

Say, "Was your card a low spade?" If the spectator chose the ♠3 he will immediately say yes. You then name the ♠3 as his card. But if the spectator chose the ♠A, he will hesitate, because aces are

Fig. 77

considered both low and high. If you spot any hesitation, smile and say, "Aces are low." Then go on to name the ♠A as his card. Turn all three cards face down and return them to the center of the deck.

82 HYPNODECK

In this routine the spectator can think of any card in the deck. The magician never knows the name of the card, yet he places the deck behind his back and instantly produces the thought-of card. The routine was devised by Howard Adams.

This is one of the few tricks in this book that require a full-deck setup, but the effect is worth the effort. After the pack has been made up, it can be reserved for use just on those occasions when you want to present this routine. Arrange the deck as follows: ♣A-♥A-♠A-♦A, then ♣2-♥2-♠2-♦2, then ♣3-♥3-♠3-♦3 and so on. The four cards of the same value are grouped together, and the suits always are in club-heart-spade-diamond order. The various four-card blocks are arranged in order, aces at the top of the deck, kings at the bottom.

With the pack thus arranged, have the spectator think of any card. Tell him to jot it down on a slip of paper. This insures against the possibility that he may forget the name of the card or that he might change his mind midway through the trick.

Deal the entire deck into two heaps, dealing from left to right. Turn your head away so you can't see the cards. Say to the spectator, "If your thought-of card is black, place the left-hand packet on my hand. Otherwise place the right-hand packet on my hand." By left-hand packet, you refer to the packet on *your* left. You can even point to it as you speak to make clear which packet you refer to.

After the spectator places the proper packet on your outstretched left hand, have him place the other packet on top of all. Square up the complete deck and face the spectator again.

Deal the deck into two heaps, dealing from left to right as before. Turn your head aside and say, "If your card was a club or a heart, place the left-hand packet on my hand. Otherwise place the right-hand packet on my hand."

After the spectator places the proper packet on your hand, have him place the remaining packet on top of all. Square the deck and place it face down in front of the spectator. Keep your head turned aside.

"I want you to deal on the table a number of cards equal to the value of your card. If you thought of the six of diamonds, for example, you would deal six cards."

After the spectator has dealt the proper number of cards, one at a time into a packet, have him place the dealt packet on top of the deck and hand you the deck behind your back.

"What was your card?" you ask. The spectator names his card. Immediately you produce the card from behind your back. It is done simply. If the above instructions were carried out correctly, the chosen card will be on top of the deck. Remove it and bring it into view.

83   RITUAL OF THE KINGS

Sometimes a simple but offbeat trick will be remembered long after more complex mysteries are forgotten. This is a strange effect, in which the spectator himself locates any card he himself names. Since there is a bit of ritual involved, the trick gains in dramatic effects if performed late at night in a dimly lit room.

To prepare, have 20 indifferent cards on top of the deck, then the four jacks, then the four kings, then the four queens and finally the balance of the deck.

Hand the spectator a piece of paper and a pencil. Ask him to think of any card in the deck. Then have him jot down the name of this card on the paper. Before he writes anything, explain that you are going to enact a ritual once associated with royalty and now carried out with picture cards.

When the spectator writes a card, make sure you see what it is. After he has done so, tell him to crumple the paper and drop it into a glass. Then place the deck in front of him. Tell him to cut the deck at about the center and complete the cut. Then have him place the card he cut to (the top card of the deck) face down on the table. Then have him cut the deck again and complete the cut.

Take the deck from him. Due to the stack in the center, the spectator must have cut to either a king, a queen or a jack. Spread the deck, locate your stack and find out which card he took. Most often, if he cut the deck at or near the center to pick a card, he will have chosen a king. Assume this is the case here. Say, "Remember, before we began I said I was going to enact a ritual with the kings. Let's use the four kings." Actually you spoke of "royalty" and "picture cards," but the spectators will think you did say kings.

Remove the three kings still in the deck plus the spectator's chosen card. Mix these four cards, glance at them, rearrange them a bit, then place the spectator's card second from the top of the packet.

Drop the supposed king packet on top of the card that the spectator placed on the table earlier. Place the rest of the deck aside. Then pick up the packet and hold it face down in the left hand.

Say, "Here is the ritual." Deal the top card to position 1 in Figure 78. Place the next card under the packet and deal the next card to position 2. Put the next card under the packet and deal the next card to position 3. Put the next card under the packet and deal the new top card to position 4. Place the remaining card in position 5 in the layout.

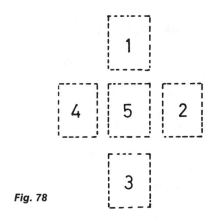

Fig. 78

Exchange cards 1 and 2, then exchange cards 3 and 4, as if it mattered to the outcome. The situation now is as shown in Figure 79. Turn up each of the cards in positions 1, 2, 3, 4, showing the four kings.

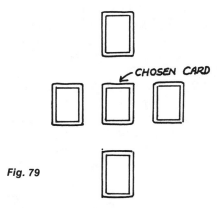

CHOSEN CARD

Fig. 79

Say, "Recall that you cut the deck randomly and removed a card. It could have been any card. Wouldn't it be interesting if the card you removed from the deck turned out to be the same as the card you wrote on that piece of paper?"

Pause and then turn up the card in the center of the layout. It is indeed the very card decided on by the spectator before the trick began!

84 DUO SPELL

By means of the remarkable principle proposed by Paul Swinford, each of two spectators locates a card mentally chosen by the other. It is worthwhile noting that at no time does the magician know either of the thought-of cards. In terms of thought-card methods this represents the apotheosis of clever thinking.

Begin by stacking 16 cards on top of the deck in the following order from the top down: ♥Q-♣6-♥2-♠J-♠8-♦K-♦3-♣4-♦J-♣10-♥A-♣Q-♠7-♦5-♦8-♠3. When ready to begin the routine, cut these 16 cards off the top. Place the top eight cards in front of the spectator on the right. Place the bottom eight cards in front of the spectator on the left.

Fan the left packet with the faces toward the spectator and ask him to think of a card. He can think of any card except the top or bottom card because, you explain, "This is to remove any suspicion that I might have you think of an obvious card." Close the fan and hold the packet face down in the left hand.

Follow the same procedure with the spectator on the right, using the other eight-card packet. After he has thought of a card, drop his packet on top of the other packet.

You are now going to perform an action known as a reverse faro. Beginning with the top card, jog every other card down. This means that you will downjog the first card, the third card, the fifth, the seventh, and so on. When you have done this, strip out the down-jogged cards and fan them before each spectator. Ask each person if he sees his card.

If both spectators answer the same (both say yes or both say no), put this packet *on top of* the other packet. If one spectator says yes and the other says no, place this packet *under* the other packet.

Explain that it takes two or three mental impressions before a clear mental picture emerges. Repeat the reverse faro described above. Remove the downjogged packet and show it to both specta-tors. As before, if both answer the same, put this packet on top of the other. If the spectators answer differently, put this packet under the other.

Repeat the above procedure one more time. Perform the reverse faro, then strip out the downjogged packet and show it to both persons. If they both see their card, put the packet on top of the other packet. Otherwise put it below the other packet.

You are now ready to conclude the effect. Downjog every other card, beginning with the top card. Strip out the downjogged packet and hand it to the spectator on the left. Give the remaining eight cards to the spectator on the right.

Ask each person to spell his card mentally, transferring a card for each letter from top to bottom. On the last letter, they place the card on the table. Each spectator includes the word "of" in the spelling. Thus if one spectator thought of the ♥2, he would spell T-W-O-O-F-H-E-A-R-T-S.

Each spectator now names his card. Turn over both of the tabled cards to show that each spectator located the *other* person's card! It is a stunning conclusion.

MIRACLES WITH ACES

In the first chapter of this book, mention was made of the importance of the opening trick in a series of card routines. Of no less importance is the closing trick. It is the last routine the audience sees and will be the one most likely to be remembered. Therefore it should be your strongest card routine.

All of the card routines in this final chapter were collected with this idea in mind. Each is suitable as a closing routine. Note that each involves the four aces because the aces impress the audience whenever they are produced or vanished. Learn the routines in this chapter and you will always finish to a round of applause.

85 FOUR-STAR ACES

Generally, the most difficult moves to perform consistently well are the second deal, the middle deal and the bottom deal. They are put to good use in this routine. The four kings are shown and dealt onto the table. On command they show up in another location. The tabled cards are turned over and prove to be the four aces.

METHOD: This fine routine was invented by Lin Searles. Secretly place the aces on top of the deck. That is the only preparation. To present the routine, run through the cards and remove the four kings. Place them in a face-up row on the table as you remove them from the deck.

Turn each king face down in place. You now have a row of four face-down kings on the table. From here on the trick proceeds at a fairly rapid pace as you say you will demonstrate middle deals and bottom deals.

Deal four cards from the top of the deck onto the leftmost king. Pick up this packet, place it on top of the deck, then deal the top card to the right, away from the king row, into a heap we'll call A.

Remove the top four cards of the deck without reversing their order. Place them on top of the next king. Pick up this packet and place it on top of the deck. Deal the top card off to the right on top of the first card you dealt, in heap A. The situation at this point is shown in Figure 80. There are two face-down kings left on the table. Two cards have been dealt off to the right in heap A.

Fig. 80   KINGS

Remove the top four cards of the deck without reversing their order. Drop them on top of the next tabled king. Pick up this packet and place it on top of the deck. Deal the top card of the deck onto heap A.

Finally, place the top four cards of the deck on top of the last king. Pick up this packet and drop it on top of the deck. Deal the topmost card of the deck onto heap A.

Say, "Where are the kings?" The spectators, thinking you used the bottom deal, will point to heap A. Say, "No, they're over here." Deal the top four cards of the deck into a face-up heap on the table to the left, revealing the four kings.

Point to the four cards in heap A and say, "I used the bottom deal, not for the kings but for the aces." Turn up the cards in heap A to show the aces. Done quickly, it is a routine that is both surprising and baffling.

86   ACE TRIUMPH

Some of the strongest card tricks substitute clever handling for sleight of hand. Once the handling is learned well enough for it to be performed without hesitation, the magic just seems to happen. In this routine face-up cards are mixed with face-down cards. The magician snaps his fingers and all the cards turn face down. The kicker is that four of the cards remain face up, but they are the four aces!

METHOD: Beforehand secretly reverse the four aces on the bottom of the deck. Thus the deck will be face down with the four aces face up on the bottom.

To perform the trick place the deck face down on the table. The long sides of the cards are parallel to the near edge of the table. Cut off the top half of the deck with the left hand, turn it face up and place it to the left of the other half of the deck. Then grasp both packets from above, as in Figure 81.

Fig. 81

Push both halves of the deck toward the center of the table. This will allow you enough room to cut the packets back toward you. Lift off about two-thirds of each half. Cross the hands and place the cut-off packets on the table as shown in Figure 82. The hands then cut off about half of these packets, the arms uncross, and the packets are placed on the table as shown in Figure 83. Note that face-up and face-down packets alternate in two rows on the table.

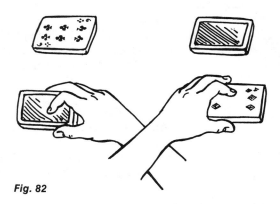

Fig. 82

Without letting go of the packets held in the hands at this point, draw them back to the near edge of the table, get the thumbs under the packets and lever them over. Place them on top of the next packets in line, as in Figure 84. The arrows in Figure 84 indicate that the packets in the hands are flipped over onto the next packets.

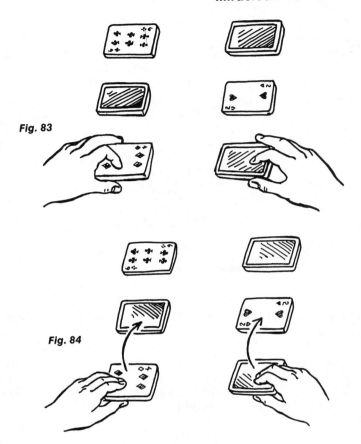

Fig. 83

Fig. 84

Slide these packets back to the near edge of the table. Get the thumbs under these packets and lever them over. Place them on top of the remaining packets, as in Figure 85. You now have just the two halves of the deck on the table. But when you do this smoothly and quickly, it appears as if face-up and face-down cards have been hopelessly mixed.

Fig. 85

Without hesitation draw the two halves of the deck back toward the near edge of the table. The right thumb slides under the right-hand packet and levers it over. Immediately riffle shuffle the two halves of the deck together, as in Figure 86. It helps if the hands are close together, covering as much of the cards as possible, so that the audience sees only the top card of each half of the deck. The illusion is that face-up and face-down cards are being shuffled together.

Fig. 86

After the shuffle, square up the deck. Give it a cut, complete the cut and turn the deck over. Snap the fingers and say, "Just like that, all the cards turn face down."

Spread the deck face down on the table. All the cards will be face down except for four face-up cards, and they are the four aces.

There is a way to obtain an additional climax with no change in the handling. Assume you are using a red-backed deck. Remove the four aces and place them aside as they will not be used. Take the four aces from a blue-backed deck and place them face up on the bottom of the face-down red-backed deck. Then on the face of a red-backed joker write, "They're marked!" Turn the joker face up and place it on the bottom of the red-backed deck.

This completes the preparation. From the top down you have the red-backed deck, then four face-up blue-backed aces, then a face-up joker on the bottom with "They're marked!" written on the face.

Perform the routine exactly as described. At the finish you will have a face-down deck with five face-up cards in the middle. Remove the joker and have the spectator read aloud the writing. Act puzzled for a moment, then turn the aces over to show that they are indeed marked, with blue ink!

87 EYEWITNESS

It is well known that the eye witnesses at the scene of a story can give conflicting testimony as to what actually happened. This is strikingly demonstrated in the following routine.

The bottom card of the deck is shown to a spectator and then dealt onto the table. This is repeated with three other spectators. When each party is asked to name his card, each names the same card. Then when the four tabled cards are turned over, none of them is the card seen by the spectators. Instead they are the four aces.

For the finish the deck is spread to show that the card they all thought they saw is reversed in the center of the pack.

METHOD: A half-card is used. As shown in Figure 87, it is half of a ♥2. Put the real ♥2 reversed in the center of the deck. Since the back of the half ♥2 is never seen, it can come from any pack. Less than a minute is needed to make up the gimmick, and the time is well spent in view of the effect that is achieved.

The half-♥2 is placed on the bottom of the deck. The four aces are placed above it. A rubber band is then snapped around the deck as shown in Figure 88.

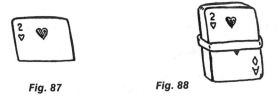

Fig. 87   **Fig. 88**

Hold the deck in the left hand so the fingers hide the ace. Display the face card to the first spectator as shown in Figure 89. Note that the fingers cover the ace that is behind the half-♥2. Lower the deck. The right fingers slide out the supposed bottom card, as in Figure 90, but instead of taking the ♥2, they take the first ace. Place this card face down on the table.

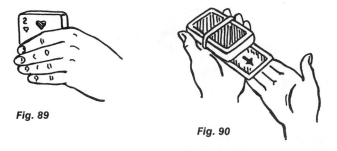

Fig. 89

Fig. 90

Put the deck behind the back, saying you are going to make a small adjustment. In fact, do nothing. Bring the deck out again and show the face card to the second spectator. He too will see the ♥2. Lower the deck, remove the bottom card (really the ace behind the half-card) and place it face down on the table. Then put the deck behind your back, saying you are going to make a small adjustment. In fact, do nothing.

Repeat the above handling with the third spectator, and repeat it again with the fourth spectator. After the fourth card has been placed face down on the table, put the deck behind the back again. Slide the half-card out from under the rubber band and quickly tuck it under the belt. Then bring the deck into view again.

Ask each person to name the card he saw on the bottom of the deck. Each will name the same card, the ♥2. It is an amusing situation because it is clear they could not possibly all have seen exactly the same card. Remove the rubber band from around the deck and spread the deck face down on the table to show the ♥2 face up in the center.

Then turn over the four cards on the table to reveal that they are the four aces.

88 WILD ACES

This is Martin Gardner's method of causing four aces to vanish from under a handkerchief and appear reversed in the center of the deck. It is one of the best tricks you can do with four aces and it requires no preparation or gimmicks.

Remove the aces from the deck and hold them in the right hand as shown in Figure 91. The left thumb and forefinger hold the deck. The other fingers grip the handkerchief as indicated in Figure 91.

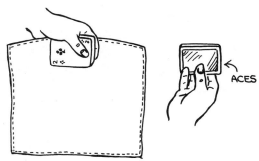

Fig. 91

The left hand remains stationary. The right hand is brought behind the handkerchief. As soon as it is hidden from the audience's view, curl the right third and fourth fingers in, bringing the aces back toward the palm, as in Figure 92.

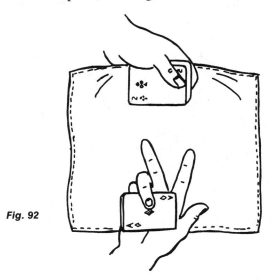

Fig. 92

The right hand moves forward under the handkerchief as if to place the aces under the cloth (see Figure 93). As the right hand moves up under the handkerchief, the aces will naturally move under the deck. It is a matter of a few minutes' practice to learn to slip the left thumb under the aces and add them onto the deck. The sequence should be smooth and rapid. It should look as if you merely placed the aces under the handkerchief.

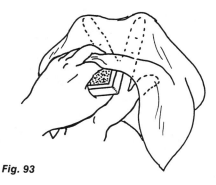

Fig. 93

Place the deck (with the aces on the bottom) face down on the table. Cut the deck and complete the cut. Announce that you will cause the aces to vanish. Snap the handkerchief away, as in Figure 94, to show that the aces are gone. Show the right hand on both sides. Then spread the deck to reveal the aces reversed in the center.

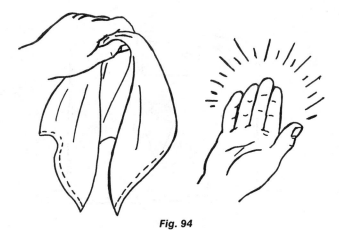

Fig. 94

A CATALOG OF SELECTED
DOVER BOOKS
IN ALL FIELDS OF INTEREST

A CATALOG OF SELECTED DOVER
BOOKS IN ALL FIELDS OF INTEREST

CONCERNING THE SPIRITUAL IN ART, Wassily Kandinsky. Pioneering work by father of abstract art. Thoughts on color theory, nature of art. Analysis of earlier masters. 12 illustrations. 80pp. of text. 5⅜ x 8½.   23411-8

ANIMALS: 1,419 Copyright-Free Illustrations of Mammals, Birds, Fish, Insects, etc., Jim Harter (ed.). Clear wood engravings present, in extremely lifelike poses, over 1,000 species of animals. One of the most extensive pictorial sourcebooks of its kind. Captions. Index. 284pp. 9 x 12.   23766-4

CELTIC ART: The Methods of Construction, George Bain. Simple geometric techniques for making Celtic interlacements, spirals, Kells-type initials, animals, humans, etc. Over 500 illustrations. 160pp. 9 x 12. (Available in U.S. only.)   22923-8

AN ATLAS OF ANATOMY FOR ARTISTS, Fritz Schider. Most thorough reference work on art anatomy in the world. Hundreds of illustrations, including selections from works by Vesalius, Leonardo, Goya, Ingres, Michelangelo, others. 593 illustrations. 192pp. 7⅛ x 10¼.   20241-0

CELTIC HAND STROKE-BY-STROKE (Irish Half-Uncial from "The Book of Kells"): An Arthur Baker Calligraphy Manual, Arthur Baker. Complete guide to creating each letter of the alphabet in distinctive Celtic manner. Covers hand position, strokes, pens, inks, paper, more. Illustrated. 48pp. 8¼ x 11.   24336-2

EASY ORIGAMI, John Montroll. Charming collection of 32 projects (hat, cup, pelican, piano, swan, many more) specially designed for the novice origami hobbyist. Clearly illustrated easy-to-follow instructions insure that even beginning papercrafters will achieve successful results. 48pp. 8¼ x 11.   27298-2

THE COMPLETE BOOK OF BIRDHOUSE CONSTRUCTION FOR WOOD-WORKERS, Scott D. Campbell. Detailed instructions, illustrations, tables. Also data on bird habitat and instinct patterns. Bibliography. 3 tables. 63 illustrations in 15 figures. 48pp. 5¼ x 8½.   24407-5

BLOOMINGDALE'S ILLUSTRATED 1886 CATALOG: Fashions, Dry Goods and Housewares, Bloomingdale Brothers. Famed merchants' extremely rare catalog depicting about 1,700 products: clothing, housewares, firearms, dry goods, jewelry, more. Invaluable for dating, identifying vintage items. Also, copyright-free graphics for artists, designers. Co-published with Henry Ford Museum & Greenfield Village. 160pp. 8¼ x 11.   25780-0

HISTORIC COSTUME IN PICTURES, Braun & Schneider. Over 1,450 costumed figures in clearly detailed engravings–from dawn of civilization to end of 19th century. Captions. Many folk costumes. 256pp. 8⅜ x 11¾.   23150-X

CATALOG OF DOVER BOOKS

STICKLEY CRAFTSMAN FURNITURE CATALOGS, Gustav Stickley and L. & J. G. Stickley. Beautiful, functional furniture in two authentic catalogs from 1910. 594 illustrations, including 277 photos, show settles, rockers, armchairs, reclining chairs, bookcases, desks, tables. 183pp. 6½ x 9¼. 23838-5

AMERICAN LOCOMOTIVES IN HISTORIC PHOTOGRAPHS: 1858 to 1949, Ron Ziel (ed.). A rare collection of 126 meticulously detailed official photographs, called "builder portraits," of American locomotives that majestically chronicle the rise of steam locomotive power in America. Introduction. Detailed captions. xi+ 129pp. 9 x 12. 27393-8

AMERICA'S LIGHTHOUSES: An Illustrated History, Francis Ross Holland, Jr. Delightfully written, profusely illustrated fact-filled survey of over 200 American lighthouses since 1716. History, anecdotes, technological advances, more. 240pp. 8 x 10¾. 25576-X

TOWARDS A NEW ARCHITECTURE, Le Corbusier. Pioneering manifesto by founder of "International School." Technical and aesthetic theories, views of industry, economics, relation of form to function, "mass-production split" and much more. Profusely illustrated. 320pp. 6⅛ x 9¼. (Available in U.S. only.) 25023-7

HOW THE OTHER HALF LIVES, Jacob Riis. Famous journalistic record, exposing poverty and degradation of New York slums around 1900, by major social reformer. 100 striking and influential photographs. 233pp. 10 x 7⅞. 22012-5

FRUIT KEY AND TWIG KEY TO TREES AND SHRUBS, William M. Harlow. One of the handiest and most widely used identification aids. Fruit key covers 120 deciduous and evergreen species; twig key 160 deciduous species. Easily used. Over 300 photographs. 126pp. 5⅜ x 8½. 20511-8

COMMON BIRD SONGS, Dr. Donald J. Borror. Songs of 60 most common U.S. birds: robins, sparrows, cardinals, bluejays, finches, more–arranged in order of increasing complexity. Up to 9 variations of songs of each species. Cassette and manual 99911-4

ORCHIDS AS HOUSE PLANTS, Rebecca Tyson Northen. Grow cattleyas and many other kinds of orchids–in a window, in a case, or under artificial light. 63 illustrations. 148pp. 5⅜ x 8½. 23261-1

MONSTER MAZES, Dave Phillips. Masterful mazes at four levels of difficulty. Avoid deadly perils and evil creatures to find magical treasures. Solutions for all 32 exciting illustrated puzzles. 48pp. 8¼ x 11. 26005-4

MOZART'S DON GIOVANNI (DOVER OPERA LIBRETTO SERIES), Wolfgang Amadeus Mozart. Introduced and translated by Ellen H. Bleiler. Standard Italian libretto, with complete English translation. Convenient and thoroughly portable–an ideal companion for reading along with a recording or the performance itself. Introduction. List of characters. Plot summary. 121pp. 5¼ x 8½. 24944-1

TECHNICAL MANUAL AND DICTIONARY OF CLASSICAL BALLET, Gail Grant. Defines, explains, comments on steps, movements, poses and concepts. 15-page pictorial section. Basic book for student, viewer. 127pp. 5⅜ x 8½. 21843-0

CATALOG OF DOVER BOOKS

THE CLARINET AND CLARINET PLAYING, David Pino. Lively, comprehensive work features suggestions about technique, musicianship, and musical interpretation, as well as guidelines for teaching, making your own reeds, and preparing for public performance. Includes an intriguing look at clarinet history. "A godsend," *The Clarinet*, Journal of the International Clarinet Society. Appendixes. 7 illus. 320pp. 5⅜ x 8½. 40270-3

HOLLYWOOD GLAMOR PORTRAITS, John Kobal (ed.). 145 photos from 1926-49. Harlow, Gable, Bogart, Bacall; 94 stars in all. Full background on photographers, technical aspects. 160pp. 8⅜ x 11¼. 23352-9

THE ANNOTATED CASEY AT THE BAT: A Collection of Ballads about the Mighty Casey/Third, Revised Edition, Martin Gardner (ed.). Amusing sequels and parodies of one of America's best-loved poems: Casey's Revenge, Why Casey Whiffed, Casey's Sister at the Bat, others. 256pp. 5⅜ x 8½. 28598-7

THE RAVEN AND OTHER FAVORITE POEMS, Edgar Allan Poe. Over 40 of the author's most memorable poems: "The Bells," "Ulalume," "Israfel," "To Helen," "The Conqueror Worm," "Eldorado," "Annabel Lee," many more. Alphabetic lists of titles and first lines. 64pp. 5³⁄₁₆ x 8¼. 26685-0

PERSONAL MEMOIRS OF U. S. GRANT, Ulysses Simpson Grant. Intelligent, deeply moving firsthand account of Civil War campaigns, considered by many the finest military memoirs ever written. Includes letters, historic photographs, maps and more. 528pp. 6⅛ x 9¼. 28587-1

ANCIENT EGYPTIAN MATERIALS AND INDUSTRIES, A. Lucas and J. Harris. Fascinating, comprehensive, thoroughly documented text describes this ancient civilization's vast resources and the processes that incorporated them in daily life, including the use of animal products, building materials, cosmetics, perfumes and incense, fibers, glazed ware, glass and its manufacture, materials used in the mummification process, and much more. 544pp. 6⅛ x 9¼. (Available in U.S. only.) 40446-3

RUSSIAN STORIES/RUSSKIE RASSKAZY: A Dual-Language Book, edited by Gleb Struve. Twelve tales by such masters as Chekhov, Tolstoy, Dostoevsky, Pushkin, others. Excellent word-for-word English translations on facing pages, plus teaching and study aids, Russian/English vocabulary, biographical/critical introductions, more. 416pp. 5⅜ x 8½. 26244-8

PHILADELPHIA THEN AND NOW: 60 Sites Photographed in the Past and Present, Kenneth Finkel and Susan Oyama. Rare photographs of City Hall, Logan Square, Independence Hall, Betsy Ross House, other landmarks juxtaposed with contemporary views. Captures changing face of historic city. Introduction. Captions. 128pp. 8¼ x 11. 25790-8

AIA ARCHITECTURAL GUIDE TO NASSAU AND SUFFOLK COUNTIES, LONG ISLAND, The American Institute of Architects, Long Island Chapter, and the Society for the Preservation of Long Island Antiquities. Comprehensive, well-researched and generously illustrated volume brings to life over three centuries of Long Island's great architectural heritage. More than 240 photographs with authoritative, extensively detailed captions. 176pp. 8¼ x 11. 26946-9

NORTH AMERICAN INDIAN LIFE: Customs and Traditions of 23 Tribes, Elsie Clews Parsons (ed.). 27 fictionalized essays by noted anthropologists examine religion, customs, government, additional facets of life among the Winnebago, Crow, Zuni, Eskimo, other tribes. 480pp. 6⅛ x 9¼. 27377-6

CATALOG OF DOVER BOOKS

FRANK LLOYD WRIGHT'S DANA HOUSE, Donald Hoffmann. Pictorial essay of residential masterpiece with over 160 interior and exterior photos, plans, elevations, sketches and studies. 128pp. 9¼ x 10¾. 29120-0

THE MALE AND FEMALE FIGURE IN MOTION: 60 Classic Photographic Sequences, Eadweard Muybridge. 60 true-action photographs of men and women walking, running, climbing, bending, turning, etc., reproduced from rare 19th-century masterpiece. vi + 121pp. 9 x 12. 24745-7

1001 QUESTIONS ANSWERED ABOUT THE SEASHORE, N. J. Berrill and Jacquelyn Berrill. Queries answered about dolphins, sea snails, sponges, starfish, fishes, shore birds, many others. Covers appearance, breeding, growth, feeding, much more. 305pp. 5¼ x 8¼. 23366-9

ATTRACTING BIRDS TO YOUR YARD, William J. Weber. Easy-to-follow guide offers advice on how to attract the greatest diversity of birds: birdhouses, feeders, water and waterers, much more. 96pp. 5³/₁₆ x 8¼. 28927-3

MEDICINAL AND OTHER USES OF NORTH AMERICAN PLANTS: A Historical Survey with Special Reference to the Eastern Indian Tribes, Charlotte Erichsen-Brown. Chronological historical citations document 500 years of usage of plants, trees, shrubs native to eastern Canada, northeastern U.S. Also complete identifying information. 343 illustrations. 544pp. 6½ x 9¼. 25951-X

STORYBOOK MAZES, Dave Phillips. 23 stories and mazes on two-page spreads: Wizard of Oz, Treasure Island, Robin Hood, etc. Solutions. 64pp. 8¼ x 11. 23628-5

AMERICAN NEGRO SONGS: 230 Folk Songs and Spirituals, Religious and Secular, John W. Work. This authoritative study traces the African influences of songs sung and played by black Americans at work, in church, and as entertainment. The author discusses the lyric significance of such songs as "Swing Low, Sweet Chariot," "John Henry," and others and offers the words and music for 230 songs. Bibliography. Index of Song Titles. 272pp. 6½ x 9¼. 40271-1

MOVIE-STAR PORTRAITS OF THE FORTIES, John Kobal (ed.). 163 glamor, studio photos of 106 stars of the 1940s: Rita Hayworth, Ava Gardner, Marlon Brando, Clark Gable, many more. 176pp. 8⅜ x 11¼. 23546-7

BENCHLEY LOST AND FOUND, Robert Benchley. Finest humor from early 30s, about pet peeves, child psychologists, post office and others. Mostly unavailable elsewhere. 73 illustrations by Peter Arno and others. 183pp. 5⅜ x 8½. 22410-4

YEKL and THE IMPORTED BRIDEGROOM AND OTHER STORIES OF YIDDISH NEW YORK, Abraham Cahan. Film Hester Street based on *Yekl* (1896). Novel, other stories among first about Jewish immigrants on N.Y.'s East Side. 240pp. 5⅜ x 8½. 22427-9

SELECTED POEMS, Walt Whitman. Generous sampling from *Leaves of Grass*. Twenty-four poems include "I Hear America Singing," "Song of the Open Road," "I Sing the Body Electric," "When Lilacs Last in the Dooryard Bloom'd," "O Captain! My Captain!"—all reprinted from an authoritative edition. Lists of titles and first lines. 128pp. 5³/₁₆ x 8¼. 26878-0

CATALOG OF DOVER BOOKS

THE BEST TALES OF HOFFMANN, E. T. A. Hoffmann. 10 of Hoffmann's most important stories: "Nutcracker and the King of Mice," "The Golden Flowerpot," etc. 458pp. 5⅜ x 8½. 21793-0

FROM FETISH TO GOD IN ANCIENT EGYPT, E. A. Wallis Budge. Rich detailed survey of Egyptian conception of "God" and gods, magic, cult of animals, Osiris, more. Also, superb English translations of hymns and legends. 240 illustrations. 545pp. 5⅜ x 8½. 25803-3

FRENCH STORIES/CONTES FRANÇAIS: A Dual-Language Book, Wallace Fowlie. Ten stories by French masters, Voltaire to Camus: "Micromegas" by Voltaire; "The Atheist's Mass" by Balzac; "Minuet" by de Maupassant; "The Guest" by Camus, six more. Excellent English translations on facing pages. Also French-English vocabulary list, exercises, more. 352pp. 5⅜ x 8½. 26443-2

CHICAGO AT THE TURN OF THE CENTURY IN PHOTOGRAPHS: 122 Historic Views from the Collections of the Chicago Historical Society, Larry A. Viskochil. Rare large-format prints offer detailed views of City Hall, State Street, the Loop, Hull House, Union Station, many other landmarks, circa 1904-1913. Introduction. Captions. Maps. 144pp. 9⅜ x 12¼. 24656-6

OLD BROOKLYN IN EARLY PHOTOGRAPHS, 1865-1929, William Lee Younger. Luna Park, Gravesend race track, construction of Grand Army Plaza, moving of Hotel Brighton, etc. 157 previously unpublished photographs. 165pp. 8⅞ x 11¾. 23587-4

THE MYTHS OF THE NORTH AMERICAN INDIANS, Lewis Spence. Rich anthology of the myths and legends of the Algonquins, Iroquois, Pawnees and Sioux, prefaced by an extensive historical and ethnological commentary. 36 illustrations. 480pp. 5⅜ x 8½. 25967-6

AN ENCYCLOPEDIA OF BATTLES: Accounts of Over 1,560 Battles from 1479 B.C. to the Present, David Eggenberger. Essential details of every major battle in recorded history from the first battle of Megiddo in 1479 B.C. to Grenada in 1984. List of Battle Maps. New Appendix covering the years 1967-1984. Index. 99 illustrations. 544pp. 6½ x 9¼. 24913-1

SAILING ALONE AROUND THE WORLD, Captain Joshua Slocum. First man to sail around the world, alone, in small boat. One of great feats of seamanship told in delightful manner. 67 illustrations. 294pp. 5⅜ x 8½. 20326-3

ANARCHISM AND OTHER ESSAYS, Emma Goldman. Powerful, penetrating, prophetic essays on direct action, role of minorities, prison reform, puritan hypocrisy, violence, etc. 271pp. 5⅜ x 8½. 22484-8

MYTHS OF THE HINDUS AND BUDDHISTS, Ananda K. Coomaraswamy and Sister Nivedita. Great stories of the epics; deeds of Krishna, Shiva, taken from puranas, Vedas, folk tales; etc. 32 illustrations. 400pp. 5⅜ x 8½. 21759-0

THE TRAUMA OF BIRTH, Otto Rank. Rank's controversial thesis that anxiety neurosis is caused by profound psychological trauma which occurs at birth. 256pp. 5⅜ x 8½. 27974-X

A THEOLOGICO-POLITICAL TREATISE, Benedict Spinoza. Also contains unfinished Political Treatise. Great classic on religious liberty, theory of government on common consent. R. Elwes translation. Total of 421pp. 5⅜ x 8½. 20249-6

CATALOG OF DOVER BOOKS

ANATOMY: A Complete Guide for Artists, Joseph Sheppard. A master of figure drawing shows artists how to render human anatomy convincingly. Over 460 illustrations. 224pp. 8⅜ x 11¼.
27279-6

MEDIEVAL CALLIGRAPHY: Its History and Technique, Marc Drogin. Spirited history, comprehensive instruction manual covers 13 styles (ca. 4th century through 15th). Excellent photographs; directions for duplicating medieval techniques with modern tools. 224pp. 8⅜ x 11¼.
26142-5

DRIED FLOWERS: How to Prepare Them, Sarah Whitlock and Martha Rankin. Complete instructions on how to use silica gel, meal and borax, perlite aggregate, sand and borax, glycerine and water to create attractive permanent flower arrangements. 12 illustrations. 32pp. 5⅜ x 8½.
21802-3

EASY-TO-MAKE BIRD FEEDERS FOR WOODWORKERS, Scott D. Campbell. Detailed, simple-to-use guide for designing, constructing, caring for and using feeders. Text, illustrations for 12 classic and contemporary designs. 96pp. 5⅜ x 8½.
25847-5

SCOTTISH WONDER TALES FROM MYTH AND LEGEND, Donald A. Mackenzie. 16 lively tales tell of giants rumbling down mountainsides, of a magic wand that turns stone pillars into warriors, of gods and goddesses, evil hags, powerful forces and more. 240pp. 5⅜ x 8½.
29677-6

THE HISTORY OF UNDERCLOTHES, C. Willett Cunnington and Phyllis Cunnington. Fascinating, well-documented survey covering six centuries of English undergarments, enhanced with over 100 illustrations: 12th-century laced-up bodice, footed long drawers (1795), 19th-century bustles, l9th-century corsets for men, Victorian "bust improvers," much more. 272pp. 5⅜ x 8¼.
27124-2

ARTS AND CRAFTS FURNITURE: The Complete Brooks Catalog of 1912, Brooks Manufacturing Co. Photos and detailed descriptions of more than 150 now very collectible furniture designs from the Arts and Crafts movement depict davenports, settees, buffets, desks, tables, chairs, bedsteads, dressers and more, all built of solid, quarter-sawed oak. Invaluable for students and enthusiasts of antiques, Americana and the decorative arts. 80pp. 6½ x 9¼.
27471-3

WILBUR AND ORVILLE: A Biography of the Wright Brothers, Fred Howard. Definitive, crisply written study tells the full story of the brothers' lives and work. A vividly written biography, unparalleled in scope and color, that also captures the spirit of an extraordinary era. 560pp. 6⅛ x 9¼.
40297-5

THE ARTS OF THE SAILOR: Knotting, Splicing and Ropework, Hervey Garrett Smith. Indispensable shipboard reference covers tools, basic knots and useful hitches; handsewing and canvas work, more. Over 100 illustrations. Delightful reading for sea lovers. 256pp. 5⅜ x 8½.
26440-8

FRANK LLOYD WRIGHT'S FALLINGWATER: The House and Its History, Second, Revised Edition, Donald Hoffmann. A total revision—both in text and illustrations—of the standard document on Fallingwater, the boldest, most personal architectural statement of Wright's mature years, updated with valuable new material from the recently opened Frank Lloyd Wright Archives. "Fascinating"—*The New York Times*. 116 illustrations. 128pp. 9¼ x 10¾.
27430-6

CATALOG OF DOVER BOOKS

PHOTOGRAPHIC SKETCHBOOK OF THE CIVIL WAR, Alexander Gardner. 100 photos taken on field during the Civil War. Famous shots of Manassas Harper's Ferry, Lincoln, Richmond, slave pens, etc. 244pp. 10⅝ x 8¼. 22731-6

FIVE ACRES AND INDEPENDENCE, Maurice G. Kains. Great back-to-the-land classic explains basics of self-sufficient farming. The one book to get. 95 illustrations. 397pp. 5⅜ x 8½. 20974-1

SONGS OF EASTERN BIRDS, Dr. Donald J. Borror. Songs and calls of 60 species most common to eastern U.S.: warblers, woodpeckers, flycatchers, thrushes, larks, many more in high-quality recording. Cassette and manual 99912-2

A MODERN HERBAL, Margaret Grieve. Much the fullest, most exact, most useful compilation of herbal material. Gigantic alphabetical encyclopedia, from aconite to zedoary, gives botanical information, medical properties, folklore, economic uses, much else. Indispensable to serious reader. 161 illustrations. 888pp. 6½ x 9¼. 2-vol. set. (Available in U.S. only.) Vol. I: 22798-7
Vol. II: 22799-5

HIDDEN TREASURE MAZE BOOK, Dave Phillips. Solve 34 challenging mazes accompanied by heroic tales of adventure. Evil dragons, people-eating plants, blood-thirsty giants, many more dangerous adversaries lurk at every twist and turn. 34 mazes, stories, solutions. 48pp. 8¼ x 11. 24566-7

LETTERS OF W. A. MOZART, Wolfgang A. Mozart. Remarkable letters show bawdy wit, humor, imagination, musical insights, contemporary musical world; includes some letters from Leopold Mozart. 276pp. 5⅜ x 8½. 22859-2

BASIC PRINCIPLES OF CLASSICAL BALLET, Agrippina Vaganova. Great Russian theoretician, teacher explains methods for teaching classical ballet. 118 illustrations. 175pp. 5⅜ x 8½. 22036-2

THE JUMPING FROG, Mark Twain. Revenge edition. The original story of The Celebrated Jumping Frog of Calaveras County, a hapless French translation, and Twain's hilarious "retranslation" from the French. 12 illustrations. 66pp. 5⅜ x 8½. 22686-7

BEST REMEMBERED POEMS, Martin Gardner (ed.). The 126 poems in this superb collection of 19th- and 20th-century British and American verse range from Shelley's "To a Skylark" to the impassioned "Renascence" of Edna St. Vincent Millay and to Edward Lear's whimsical "The Owl and the Pussycat." 224pp. 5⅜ x 8½. 27165-X

COMPLETE SONNETS, William Shakespeare. Over 150 exquisite poems deal with love, friendship, the tyranny of time, beauty's evanescence, death and other themes in language of remarkable power, precision and beauty. Glossary of archaic terms. 80pp. 5³⁄₁₆ x 8¼. 26686-9

THE BATTLES THAT CHANGED HISTORY, Fletcher Pratt. Eminent historian profiles 16 crucial conflicts, ancient to modern, that changed the course of civilization. 352pp. 5⅜ x 8½. 41129-X

THE WIT AND HUMOR OF OSCAR WILDE, Alvin Redman (ed.). More than 1,000 ripostes, paradoxes, wisecracks: Work is the curse of the drinking classes; I can resist everything except temptation; etc. 258pp. 5⅜ x 8½. 20602-5

SHAKESPEARE LEXICON AND QUOTATION DICTIONARY, Alexander Schmidt. Full definitions, locations, shades of meaning in every word in plays and poems. More than 50,000 exact quotations. 1,485pp. 6½ x 9¼. 2-vol. set.
Vol. 1: 22726-X
Vol. 2: 22727-8

SELECTED POEMS, Emily Dickinson. Over 100 best-known, best-loved poems by one of America's foremost poets, reprinted from authoritative early editions. No comparable edition at this price. Index of first lines. 64pp. 5³⁄₁₆ x 8¼. 26466-1

THE INSIDIOUS DR. FU-MANCHU, Sax Rohmer. The first of the popular mystery series introduces a pair of English detectives to their archnemesis, the diabolical Dr. Fu-Manchu. Flavorful atmosphere, fast-paced action, and colorful characters enliven this classic of the genre. 208pp. 5³⁄₁₆ x 8¼. 29898-1

THE MALLEUS MALEFICARUM OF KRAMER AND SPRENGER, translated by Montague Summers. Full text of most important witchhunter's "bible," used by both Catholics and Protestants. 278pp. 6⅝ x 10. 22802-9

SPANISH STORIES/CUENTOS ESPAÑOLES: A Dual-Language Book, Angel Flores (ed.). Unique format offers 13 great stories in Spanish by Cervantes, Borges, others. Faithful English translations on facing pages. 352pp. 5⅜ x 8½. 25399-6

GARDEN CITY, LONG ISLAND, IN EARLY PHOTOGRAPHS, 1869–1919, Mildred H. Smith. Handsome treasury of 118 vintage pictures, accompanied by carefully researched captions, document the Garden City Hotel fire (1899), the Vanderbilt Cup Race (1908), the first airmail flight departing from the Nassau Boulevard Aerodrome (1911), and much more. 96pp. 8⅞ x 11¾. 40669-5

OLD QUEENS, N.Y., IN EARLY PHOTOGRAPHS, Vincent F. Seyfried and William Asadorian. Over 160 rare photographs of Maspeth, Jamaica, Jackson Heights, and other areas. Vintage views of DeWitt Clinton mansion, 1939 World's Fair and more. Captions. 192pp. 8⅞ x 11. 26358-4

CAPTURED BY THE INDIANS: 15 Firsthand Accounts, 1750-1870, Frederick Drimmer. Astounding true historical accounts of grisly torture, bloody conflicts, relentless pursuits, miraculous escapes and more, by people who lived to tell the tale. 384pp. 5⅜ x 8½. 24901-8

THE WORLD'S GREAT SPEECHES (Fourth Enlarged Edition), Lewis Copeland, Lawrence W. Lamm, and Stephen J. McKenna. Nearly 300 speeches provide public speakers with a wealth of updated quotes and inspiration–from Pericles' funeral oration and William Jennings Bryan's "Cross of Gold Speech" to Malcolm X's powerful words on the Black Revolution and Earl of Spenser's tribute to his sister, Diana, Princess of Wales. 944pp. 5⅜ x 8⅜. 40903-1

THE BOOK OF THE SWORD, Sir Richard F. Burton. Great Victorian scholar/adventurer's eloquent, erudite history of the "queen of weapons"–from prehistory to early Roman Empire. Evolution and development of early swords, variations (sabre, broadsword, cutlass, scimitar, etc.), much more. 336pp. 6⅛ x 9¼.
25434-8

CATALOG OF DOVER BOOKS

AUTOBIOGRAPHY: The Story of My Experiments with Truth, Mohandas K. Gandhi. Boyhood, legal studies, purification, the growth of the Satyagraha (nonviolent protest) movement. Critical, inspiring work of the man responsible for the freedom of India. 480pp. 5⅜ x 8½. (Available in U.S. only.)   24593-4

CELTIC MYTHS AND LEGENDS, T. W. Rolleston. Masterful retelling of Irish and Welsh stories and tales. Cuchulain, King Arthur, Deirdre, the Grail, many more. First paperback edition. 58 full-page illustrations. 512pp. 5⅜ x 8½.   26507-2

THE PRINCIPLES OF PSYCHOLOGY, William James. Famous long course complete, unabridged. Stream of thought, time perception, memory, experimental methods; great work decades ahead of its time. 94 figures. 1,391pp. 5⅜ x 8½. 2-vol. set.
Vol. I: 20381-6   Vol. II: 20382-4

THE WORLD AS WILL AND REPRESENTATION, Arthur Schopenhauer. Definitive English translation of Schopenhauer's life work, correcting more than 1,000 errors, omissions in earlier translations. Translated by E. F. J. Payne. Total of 1,269pp. 5⅜ x 8½. 2-vol. set.
Vol. 1: 21761-2   Vol. 2: 21762-0

MAGIC AND MYSTERY IN TIBET, Madame Alexandra David-Neel. Experiences among lamas, magicians, sages, sorcerers, Bonpa wizards. A true psychic discovery. 32 illustrations. 321pp. 5⅜ x 8½. (Available in U.S. only.)   22682-4

THE EGYPTIAN BOOK OF THE DEAD, E. A. Wallis Budge. Complete reproduction of Ani's papyrus, finest ever found. Full hieroglyphic text, interlinear transliteration, word-for-word translation, smooth translation. 533pp. 6½ x 9¼.   21866-X

MATHEMATICS FOR THE NONMATHEMATICIAN, Morris Kline. Detailed, college-level treatment of mathematics in cultural and historical context, with numerous exercises. Recommended Reading Lists. Tables. Numerous figures. 641pp. 5⅜ x 8½.   24823-2

PROBABILISTIC METHODS IN THE THEORY OF STRUCTURES, Isaac Elishakoff. Well-written introduction covers the elements of the theory of probability from two or more random variables, the reliability of such multivariable structures, the theory of random function, Monte Carlo methods of treating problems incapable of exact solution, and more. Examples. 502pp. 5⅜ x 8½.   40691-1

THE RIME OF THE ANCIENT MARINER, Gustave Doré, S. T. Coleridge. Doré's finest work; 34 plates capture moods, subtleties of poem. Flawless full-size reproductions printed on facing pages with authoritative text of poem. "Beautiful. Simply beautiful."—*Publisher's Weekly.* 77pp. 9¼ x 12.   22305-1

NORTH AMERICAN INDIAN DESIGNS FOR ARTISTS AND CRAFTSPEOPLE, Eva Wilson. Over 360 authentic copyright-free designs adapted from Navajo blankets, Hopi pottery, Sioux buffalo hides, more. Geometrics, symbolic figures, plant and animal motifs, etc. 128pp. 8⅜ x 11. (Not for sale in the United Kingdom.)   25341-4

SCULPTURE: Principles and Practice, Louis Slobodkin. Step-by-step approach to clay, plaster, metals, stone; classical and modern. 253 drawings, photos. 255pp. 8⅛ x 11.   22960-2

THE INFLUENCE OF SEA POWER UPON HISTORY, 1660–1783, A. T. Mahan. Influential classic of naval history and tactics still used as text in war colleges. First paperback edition. 4 maps. 24 battle plans. 640pp. 5⅜ x 8½.   25509-3

THE STORY OF THE TITANIC AS TOLD BY ITS SURVIVORS, Jack Winocour (ed.). What it was really like. Panic, despair, shocking inefficiency, and a little heroism. More thrilling than any fictional account. 26 illustrations. 320pp. 5⅜ x 8½. 20610-6

FAIRY AND FOLK TALES OF THE IRISH PEASANTRY, William Butler Yeats (ed.). Treasury of 64 tales from the twilight world of Celtic myth and legend: "The Soul Cages," "The Kildare Pooka," "King O'Toole and his Goose," many more. Introduction and Notes by W. B. Yeats. 352pp. 5⅜ x 8½. 26941-8

BUDDHIST MAHAYANA TEXTS, E. B. Cowell and others (eds.). Superb, accurate translations of basic documents in Mahayana Buddhism, highly important in history of religions. The Buddha-karita of Asvaghosha, Larger Sukhavativyuha, more. 448pp. 5⅜ x 8½. 25552-2

ONE TWO THREE . . . INFINITY: Facts and Speculations of Science, George Gamow. Great physicist's fascinating, readable overview of contemporary science: number theory, relativity, fourth dimension, entropy, genes, atomic structure, much more. 128 illustrations. Index. 352pp. 5⅜ x 8½. 25664-2

EXPERIMENTATION AND MEASUREMENT, W. J. Youden. Introductory manual explains laws of measurement in simple terms and offers tips for achieving accuracy and minimizing errors. Mathematics of measurement, use of instruments, experimenting with machines. 1994 edition. Foreword. Preface. Introduction. Epilogue. Selected Readings. Glossary. Index. Tables and figures. 128pp. 5⅜ x 8½. 40451-X

DALÍ ON MODERN ART: The Cuckolds of Antiquated Modern Art, Salvador Dalí. Influential painter skewers modern art and its practitioners. Outrageous evaluations of Picasso, Cézanne, Turner, more. 15 renderings of paintings discussed. 44 calligraphic decorations by Dalí. 96pp. 5⅜ x 8½. (Available in U.S. only.) 29220-7

ANTIQUE PLAYING CARDS: A Pictorial History, Henry René D'Allemagne. Over 900 elaborate, decorative images from rare playing cards (14th–20th centuries): Bacchus, death, dancing dogs, hunting scenes, royal coats of arms, players cheating, much more. 96pp. 9¼ x 12¼. 29265-7

MAKING FURNITURE MASTERPIECES: 30 Projects with Measured Drawings, Franklin H. Gottshall. Step-by-step instructions, illustrations for constructing handsome, useful pieces, among them a Sheraton desk, Chippendale chair, Spanish desk, Queen Anne table and a William and Mary dressing mirror. 224pp. 8⅛ x 11¼. 29338-6

THE FOSSIL BOOK: A Record of Prehistoric Life, Patricia V. Rich et al. Profusely illustrated definitive guide covers everything from single-celled organisms and dinosaurs to birds and mammals and the interplay between climate and man. Over 1,500 illustrations. 760pp. 7½ x 10⅛. 29371-8

Paperbound unless otherwise indicated. Available at your book dealer, online at **www.doverpublications.com**, or by writing to Dept. GI, Dover Publications, Inc., 31 East 2nd Street, Mineola, NY 11501. For current price information or for free catalogues (please indicate field of interest), write to Dover Publications or log on to **www.doverpublications.com** and see every Dover book in print. Dover publishes more than 500 books each year on science, elementary and advanced mathematics, biology, music, art, literary history, social sciences, and other areas.

2008 ✓